W9-DBH-594

FULL PRICE

FULL PRICE

COMPETING
ON VALUE IN THE
NEW ECONOMY

Thomas J. Winninger

DEARBORN™
TRADE
A **Kaplan Professional** Company

This publication is designed to provide accurate and authoritative information in regard to the subject matter covered. It is sold with the understanding that the publisher is not engaged in rendering legal, accounting, or other professional service. If legal advice or other expert assistance is required, the services of a competent professional person should be sought.

Senior Acquisitions Editor: Jean Iversen Cook
Senior Managing Editor: Jack Kiburz
Interior Design: Lucy Jenkins
Cover Design: Design Solutions
Typesetting: the dotted i

Library of Congress Cataloging-in-Publication Data
Winninger, Thomas J.
 Full price : competing on value in the new economy / Thomas J. Winninger.
  p. cm.
 Includes index.
 ISBN 0-7931-3954-6
  1. Quality of products. 2. Consumer satisfaction. 3. Prices. 4. Value.
 5. Competition. I. Title.
 HF5415.157.W56 2000
 658.8'16—dc21

                    00-009401

Dearborn Trade books are available at special quantity discounts to use as premiums and sales promotions, or for use in corporate training programs. For more information, please call the Special Sales Manager at 800-621-9621, ext. 4514, or write to Dearborn Financial Publishing, Inc., 155 North Wacker Drive, Chicago, IL 60606-1719.

BOOKS BY THE AUTHOR

CONTENTS

PREFACE

The unbelievably competitive nature of almost every industry in America is forcing companies—big and small—to fight harder for slimmer margins while battling even more to seemingly stay afloat. The effects of globalization and deregulation coupled with the preeminent rise of the consumer through the rise of the Internet are increasingly contributing to the difficulty businesses have in getting full price for their products and services. Consumers are loyal so long as they can pay the lowest price. Far too often, loyalty disappears as soon as a competitor is able to do it cheaper. Frustratingly, many companies find themselves in a descending spiral where it seems the only way to do business is to almost give it away.

Fortunately, it doesn't have to be this way. In the following pages, I will show you in a straightforward, yet powerful way how companies have been able to get away from fruitless price wars and move toward achieving *full price* for their products and services. The companies described here are leaders in creating and implementing time-proven strategies that truly set them apart from the rest of the marketplace.

One of the most compelling issues I deal with is how companies need to address their destinations in light of the revolutionary technological advances of today. The Internet and the proliferation of information technology are forcing business leaders to look at themselves and their markets in completely new and revolutionary ways. The companies who will thrive in the new century are the ones who best harness technology and unleash its power to enhance the already existing relationships with their best customers. Doing so will ensure that companies are able to get full price for what they sell.

This book celebrates the notion that any company, regardless of where it stands today, can build the critical relationships and processes needed to attain full price. The imperatives put forth here provide you, the reader, with the pillars on which to construct that foundation. It is my hope that you will follow this blueprint so that your company can get out of the vicious cycle of constantly cutting your prices and instead arrive at full price.

—Thom Winninger
Founder, Winninger Institute for Market Strategy

INTRODUCTION

As we begin the new millennium, the 21st century will undoubtedly provide the greatest economic opportunities for more Americans than ever before. Never in recorded history will so many people in one place live so well. The fantastic system afforded by a delicate balance of individual liberty and free enterprise has opened the door to the foremost wealth-building opportunities ever known to humankind.

In the past century, America twice liberated Europe from tyranny, saved Asia from utter destruction, put a man on the moon, defeated communism, and spread freedom and prosperity to the four corners of the globe. The unprecedented rise in per capita income and personal freedom throughout the world is a triumph of American values and principles.

Instant communication and fantastic transportation systems have brought the world closer than ever before. E-mail needs only milliseconds to be sent halfway around the world. Air travel allows for the movement of goods and people in hours instead of weeks or months. As the undisputed leader of technological innovation, a tremendous demand for American knowledge and expertise exists all over the planet. Like the 20th century, the 21st century will certainly again be "the American century."

In addition, the demand for skilled workers and specialized products is increasing, while discretionary spending and consumption are at all-time high levels. There is no better time than now to get full price for your product or service. In short, these should be the "good old days."

Wall Street informs us that corporate profits continue to remain flat while corporate revenues are said to be higher than ever before. The U.S. Department of Commerce reported early in 2000 that of the approximately 20,000 new products entering the marketplace that year, more than 80 percent, or 18,000, will fail. Blatantly put, there is hardly anyone in the richest, most dynamic economy in the world who is getting full price for their goods and service.

The examples of this national dilemma are rampant throughout the country: A business owner working harder than anytime in her life and still not earning a decent living. A salesman selling more product year after year and bringing home less and less. A midsize company manufacturing and distributing more of its product each quarter and barely making a profit.

The vast majority of American companies are simply not maximizing all of the resources at their disposal in order to charge—and receive—full price for their product or service. They follow the same cookie-cutter formulas for bringing them closer to what they think they're really worth. Setting up a Web site, giving better payment terms to customers, and cutting prices are all standard, acceptable ways of conducting business in today's marketplace. Nevertheless, if you do what everyone else does, you may never get what you're worth.

It is necessary to reinvent the ways in which American companies can achieve their goals. The new economy of the 21st century requires that you set yourself apart from the rest of the marketplace—to stand out from the crowd, to be the market leader, to create a niche, to build a brand for your product or service.

The Internet and the speed with which consumers can obtain pricing information is revolutionizing the relationship between buyer and seller. Real-time quotes, "bot shopping," and dealer invoices are merely a mouse-click away. Because of the Web and the new power it gives consumers, companies are encountering customers who know more about their core business, their costs, and their prices than ever before.

Fortunately, there is a way for companies to reallocate the resources at their disposal and get what their products and services are worth. It is not necessary to invest more money or time in order to achieve full price. It is already within reach. All you have to do is redistribute your assets and reevaluate your planning. The results can be fantastic. It will be possible for you and your company to achieve maximum value for your product or service, thereby achieving full price for your product or service.

Hundreds of books and dozens of experts tell Americans the road to getting what they or their product is really worth is through negotiation. Although negotiation is an important skill, it is not the method by which to achieve full price. In today's ultracompetitive marketplace, negotiation is—more often than not—just another technique for lowering the price. Negotiation ultimately diminishes the value of the product or service in question. Yet, unbelievably, for a large number of American companies, negotiation is still the preferred method for conducting business.

Success in the 21st century will not be attainable by winning price wars over your competition or through negotiating your way to the top. Success will be achieved by creating a value for your service or product that demands full price. Lexus, Tommy Hilfiger, Ritz-Carlton, Dom Perignon, Michael Jordan, and Giorgio Armani are all well-known examples of companies that have created a value that allows them to *ask for* and, more important, *get* what their products or services are really worth.

The good news is that you can repackage your products and services to receive full price. Whether your company has 10 employees or 100,000, it is possible to get what you're really worth.

The strategies spelled out in this book will show you how to achieve full price for your product or service. All of the information presented here comes from my nearly 25 years of experience in helping some of America's finest companies maximize their value.

At one time or another, each of my clients was faced with the same scenario: increased output, rising revenues, and falling margins. Each was doing more and earning less. This vicious cycle seems never ending, especially in the price-driven environment of today. Yet, there is a way out. You can do something about it.

By applying the universal principles set forth here, I am quite certain you, too, can get what your products or services are really worth. It is not terribly difficult, but it will require a new way of looking at your company and what you do.

CHAPTER 1

Maximum Value Perception

> *"The key to life is one thing."*
> —Curly, as played by Jack Palance,
> to Billy Crystal in the movie *City Slickers*

After nearly 25 years of working with hundreds of America's finest companies, I am firmly convinced the only way to achieve long-term market dominance with high margins is by creating value. There is no other way. Excellence can be achieved solely by steadily building value into your product or service.

The most successful companies today—the market leaders—are built on differentiation. In other words, they offer customers something of value that sets their product or service apart from the competition. Being above the crowd creates a value that makes it possible for them to get what they're really worth.

FOCUS ON "ONE THING"

In most cases, success can be attributed primarily to, as Curly says in *City Slickers*, "one thing." At Disney, it's "magic." At Volvo, it's "safety." Domino's Pizza's one thing was "30 minutes or less." Kal-Kan's is a "happy pet." Kodak's is "image management."

Unfortunately, the vast majority of American businesses tend to concentrate their energies on price and/or cost rather than on their one thing. Most competitive brands rarely differ from each other in any substantial way. As a result, price becomes the crucial determinant in the buying decision, and this inevitably leads to a price war.

In a price war, the only goal is survival. Nobody wins. A price war encourages customers to focus only on the product's price tag, not its value or benefits. Moreover, customers *always* remember the lowest price. The net outcome of a price war is an industry in which revenues and profits are damaged for years to come. The medical profession, the personal computer industry, mortgage companies, and pizza chains have all recently undergone major price wars. The casualties are gone and buried. The survivors are shell-shocked— wandering aimlessly, trying to figure out how it happened and what to do next. However, there is hope. It is possible to break out of the insanity of focusing only on price. It is conceivable to increase your company's volume *and* profits.

This book will detail my proven formula for how to stand out and achieve full price: how to find your one thing and capitalize on it. *The great news is that finding your one thing may not cost you a lot of money.* All you need to do is rethink and retool your company's approach to the marketplace. Doing so will become a turning point for your company and its position in the marketplace.

DEFINING MAXIMUM VALUE PERCEPTION

Maximum Value Perception, or MVP as it is called, is defined as seeking and fulfilling the highest need of your premium customer. Doing so creates a value that demands full price. MVP is a universal principle. It is what successful companies use to create value in products and services, to differentiate themselves in the marketplace, to get closer to what they call utopia, or that full-price figure.

It is critical that Maximum Value Perception be thoroughly defined:

Seeking is synonymous with explore, venture, inquire. You take it upon yourself to seek what people really want from you.

And is a conjunction that joins the two activities seeking and fulfilling. They go hand in hand; one without the other is inadequate.

Fulfilling is similar to carry out, realize, and complete. It signifies finality: mission accomplished.

Highest is the same as supreme, *preeminent,* and *uppermost.* Nothing is greater.

Need is a requirement, necessity, or exigency. It is the basis for survival.

Premium is synonymous with superior, prime, and select: the best of the best.

Customer is the entity that buys your product or service.

Again, Maximum Value Perception is seeking and fulfilling the highest need of your premium customer. For Nordstrom it is "high quality." For Southwest Airlines it is "easy flyer." From my definition, four questions jump out, demanding further explanation. They are:

1. Who is my premium customer?
2. What is my premium customer's highest need?
3. How do I determine my Maximum Value Perception?
4. How do I achieve Maximum Value Perception and receive full price?

The rest of this chapter will answer questions 1, 2, and 3. The remainder of the book will deal with question 4 and illustrate proven strategies on how to get what your products or services are really worth.

Your Premium Customer

The premium customer is marked by four characteristics surrounding you, your product, or service:

1. The premium customer has a high-level need for your product or service. They view your product or service as an essential element of their performance.
2. The premium customer has a unique value need for your product. They understand and agree with the value of the one thing you do. Further, if they do not understand, they are capable of being educated as to what makes you, your product, or your service unique.
3. The premium customer has a frequent need for your product. They are not a one-time sale. An insurance agent might view his premium customer as that client who purchases not only life insurance from him but also fire, auto, and home insurance. A car dealership may reason its premium customer is the buyer who acquires not only a car but also brings the vehicle in for regular servicing.
4. The premium customer is an "influencer" of others. They impact in a positive way the actions and beliefs of others about your company's products and services. The premium customer is the best customer for your product.

Your Premium Customer's Highest Need

To seek the highest need of the premium customer, you need to identify the one thing that makes you special.

In my definition of Maximum Value Perception, *seeking* is intimately connected to the highest need of our premium customer. It demands something be done.

Seeking is a proactive word calling us to action. It is the direct opposite of the retail mentality. Companies with a retail outlook say, "If customers want something, they will find us, ask us to do it." Such companies react to their customers. Retailers expect something to happen. They sit around and wait for the phone to ring or the customer to walk in the door. The proactive company, on the other hand, seizes the initiative and is always moving forward.

Ask questions of your premium customers. Investigate what these people need. What do they value? The adage, "If you want to be successful in you career, be around successful people," is quite applicable. If you want your business to succeed, hang out with successful customers. Interact with them. Focus on what makes them tick. By hearing right from the horse's mouth exactly what they need, you can begin to focus your product or service on the one thing that makes you unique to them.

Learn to ask specific questions of your premium customers. Qualify your research. Do not ask, "How am I doing?" Instead, find out what the one thing is that will get somebody to drive the wrong way up a one-way street to see me? Jack Welch, CEO of General Electric, advises you to "find out the one thing that gets in the way of your customers buying from you, then eliminate it."

Bill Clinton's presidential campaign in 1992 is a perfect example of seeking the premium customer's highest need. In the face of George Bush's record-high popularity following the Gulf War, the Clinton campaign, through intense, qualified investigation, identified the highest need of likely voters to be the future of the economy. The campaign's mantra became "It's the economy, stupid." For months, even while he was way behind in the polls, Clinton focused on one thing—the economy. Eventually, after the fervor of the victory in the Gulf died down, voters came to believe Clinton, and Clinton alone could be trusted with the economic future of their children and the country. Clinton was perceived by the electorate to "own" the issue of the economy. For those Americans whose highest need was economic certainty in an uncertain world, Bill Clinton was the only real choice.

DETERMINING AND ACHIEVING
MAXIMUM VALUE PERCEPTION

To achieve Maximum Value Perception, we have to maximize something. For our purposes we need to address the following: Who are you? What are you doing? Who are you doing "it" for? What makes you unique? By answering these questions, it will become much easier to implement the time-proven strategies presented in the remainder of this book and achieve full price for yourself and your product or service.

Who Are You?

Volvo is "safety." Toro is "a beautiful yard." The hardware store around the corner from my home is "the guys who make weekend jobs easier." McDonald's is "fast food."

All of these are examples of "who they are." Each is defined by its one thing.

What Are You Doing?

Beyond understanding exactly who you are, it is equally important to realize specifically what makes you number one at what you do. What is the process that makes you who you are? It is an expanded definition of who you are.

Volvo is "safety" because it ensures that everything inside and outside of its automobiles is made of the highest-quality materials.

Toro is "a beautiful yard" because it offers the finest selection of lawn equipment to the residential homeowner.

The Ace Hardware store around the corner is "the guys who make weekend jobs easier" because someone always greets me at the door and helps me with whatever project I am working on.

McDonald's is "fast food" because it can get a hamburger off the grill and into the bag faster.

Who Are You Doing It For?

A fundamental reality of business today is that all customers are not equal. Unfortunately, today's marketplace finds companies trying to deal with several different types of customer in relatively the same way. The results are predictable: a small percentage of your clients demanding an increasing amount of your time at the expense of the others. Over the past three decades, my work with many of America's leading companies has led me to conclude that most businesses have three different types of customer: (1) the "custom," (2) the "vacillating," and (3) the "standard."

The "paradigm of commodity value," as I call it, finds the three types of customers delineated in the following manner: 17 percent are custom; 56 percent are vacillating; and 27 percent are standard.

Custom clients tend to be about 17 percent of all of your customers. They are the premium customers. They depend upon you for everything surrounding your product or service. In addition to buying the product, premium customers purchase all of the elements related to it, such as service and installation. They are usually willing to pay full price. The custom, or premium, customers might not be your biggest clients. They are, however, usually your best. They are wonderful people.

Vacillating customers typically make up about 56 percent of your clientele. These are customers who have no idea what they are about. They constantly vacillate between the low end and the high end of the buying spectrum. Unfortunately, few businesses take the time to educate them. On Saturday they shop for clothes at K-Mart and on Sunday they are at Brooks Brothers. They are confused.

Standard customers make up approximately 27 percent of your total buyers. These customers are price driven. They will never appreciate your work. They shop around for the best deal and constantly beat you up on price. They are coupon clippers. They buy from you only because you have the best price today for the commodity they want today. They have no allegiance to you or your product or service. If they find a better price, they're gone in a minute. They eat up your limited resources and generate little, if any, revenue or profit. They generally cause more problems than they are worth.

I am convinced that as you were reading these descriptions, you could easily place most of your customers into one of these categories. To move closer to getting what your product or service is really worth, the objective is twofold: (1) to shift as many of your customers as possible from the standard and vacillating categories to the custom one, and (2) to constantly purify your focus—keeping your custom customers customized.

For decades, McDonald's was the strongest fast-food company in the world. Generations of people all over the world identified McDonald's as the best place to get food in a hurry. McDonald's market dominance soared and profits skyrocketed. However, in the late 1980s, despite year after year of unprecedented success using the same formula, McDonald's decided to change and become a "food-fast" company. Management believed it could increase business by offering a wider variety of food products. Unfortunately, sales fell and profits plummeted. Customers ran away as fast as they could to Wendy's and Burger King.

What happened? McDonald's had lost focus on the one thing that made it unique to its premium customer. The ability to deliver a meal in less than 90 seconds met the highest need of millions of people who came to identify McDonald's as the fastest way to fill their stomachs. Except for the french fries, nobody ever raved about the taste or quality of McDonald's food. It was always the service. When food replaced service as the primary reason to go to McDonald's, millions of customers left. They could get a better hamburger somewhere else.

What Makes You Unique?

The "Rule of Five" contains five items that make you unique to your premium customers. The first three are tangible: response, knowledge, and quality. The other two are discretionary for you to discover from your unique premium customers.

Response. As Mom used to say, first impressions are the most important. In today's rapid-paced world, response is the way you create a first impression. It is a decisive component of what makes you unique today. Increasingly, more than anything else companies are judged by how soon they respond to a customer's inquiry or request.

It is crucial to understand that response only for the sake of response is vacuous. Response needs to be properly framed within the customer's expectancy level. The rule is simple: always meet the expectancy or beat it. Progressive Insurance of Cleveland has a mobile fleet of adjusters that arrives at the accident scene to complete the claim on sight.

A word of caution, however. You do not want to redefine an expectancy that down the road you're going to have trouble meeting. The gap between expectancy and reality is sometimes called frustration.

Knowledge. What do you know? What information do you possess that is important to your customer? What do you know your customer doesn't know? In my work with Trek Bicycle dealers, I found many dealers who possessed no critical, integrated knowledge of the product they were selling. They knew they were offering a two-wheeled vehicle powered by human energy—nothing else. Customers all over of the country were telling dealers, "Don't sell me a bicycle if you can't tell me where I can ride it and, more important, how I can improve my overall riding experience." A simple solution was to give every customer a map detailing riding areas in the vicinity of the store. Bose educates each customer that purchases its surround-sound stereo on how to properly install the system through the use of videotapes and 24-hour 800 numbers.

Hertz learned its customers were much less interested in renting a car than with getting to their destination. Global positioning systems, detailed maps, and helpful customer service attendants all make it easier and less stressful for Hertz customers to get to their ultimate destination. Such knowledge is critical to customers who have no idea how to get around a city they are unfamiliar with.

Quality of your product or service. Application of your product to its highest need is essential to making you unique. Individuals working with a large firm need to deliver what they know to be a specific need of their customer—their boss.

My work with Stihl led us to find that Stihl chainsaws were considered to be of the highest quality and most durable in the marketplace. To substantiate the price difference between a Stihl and other brands, we created a program that educated Stihl dealers to focus on the quality and availability of their chainsaws. A Stihl would likely last at least six years under normal operating conditions —several years longer than the competition. By having the customer view the relatively small price difference in terms of years, the quality of the product could command full price.

Discretionary items. The last two items that make your product or service unique are discretionary. They cannot be pinned down. They vary from company to company. Do you like the person you bought it from? What is the level of personal convenience? Do you like the color? What about the product specifications?

Even if you don't know what these discretionary items are, your premium customers do. Simply ask them. You might be very surprised by what you learn.

SUMMARY

Until the product is delivered and the customer has the product in hand, everything the customer is operating on is perception. The challenge for us is to make what we do tangible: to turn the perception into the highest possible reality—*to do one thing.*

Maximum Value Perception, or MVP, is seeking and fulfilling the highest need of your premium customer. MVP asks and answers the following questions:

- Who are you?

- What do you know?

- Who do you do it for?

- What makes you unique?

CHAPTER 2

Leading
the Field

"We define a leading brand's true strength based on its ability to command a premium price."

—Roberto Goizueta, former chairman of Coca-Cola

It is incumbent today for a business to understand and appeal to what its customers actually value. It is critical for survival in the new economy. To get what your product or service is worth, it is necessary to identify and provide a "customer-defined experience." The leaders in their industries do exactly that. In leading the field, companies develop innovative ways to implement a customer-focused strategy based on the highest needs of their premium customers. In other words, leaders learn what the highest needs are and deliver to that level.

Robert Eckert, president and CEO of Kraft Foods, doesn't rest easy. He spends his days and nights working on turning Kraft into what Microsoft is to the software business, Nike to running shoes, and Disney to family entertainment. That is his greatest challenge. Who knows that Kraft makes Jell-O, Maxwell House, Kool-Aid, and Cool Whip? Yet 90 percent of Americans use these products, so Kraft is well positioned to relay to consumers who it is and what it stands for. What customers see from Kraft are communications that show Kraft understands their values and is uniquely able to make the connections that are so important to them.

Eckert speaks for literally millions of American companies when he identifies complacency as the real issue. There are essentially three kinds of companies: companies that do well; companies that follow those that are doing well; and the outsiders who change things, become very successful, and gradually replace the leaders. Kraft wants to be in the last group. To get what you're truly worth, you need to be in the last group as well.

The highest-paid actor in film history is not Arnold Schwarzenegger, Sylvester Stallone, or Bruce Willis. It is Adam Sandler. The former *Saturday Night Live* regular is by no means on the same acting level as Tom Hanks, Harrison Ford, or Gene Hackman. His most recent films—*The Wedding Singer, Happy Chandler, The Waterboy,* and *Big Daddy*—are not among the highest-grossing pictures nor do they offer much of an artistic statement.

Nevertheless, Sandler leads the field by fulfilling the highest need of his premium customer—the Hollywood studios. The motion picture industry has determined that the vast majority of its present and future domestic revenues are intricately tied to the group between 15 and 24 years of age. By capturing this critical demographic, the Hollywood studios can be certain of guaranteed revenues well into the next century. Adam Sandler, the most popular actor with young moviegoers, goes a long way to help the film industry achieve its goals. And because of this, he creates a value for himself that demands full price.

To lead the field in your particular industry, it is critical to attach yourself to your customers while keeping an eye on your competition—that is, to identify the one thing that sets you apart from everyone else in the eyes of your premium customers. Successful companies and individuals implement strategies that allow them to lead the field—to be the followed rather than those who follow. Their strategies include building an advisory board; branding themselves, their product, or service; and benchmarking their process.

However, a substantial number of companies foolishly pay the vast majority of their attention to their competitors. It is an all too common occurrence. As a result, customer satisfaction in the United

States is at an all-time low. When companies talk to their customers about their product or service, praise is rarely given. For the most part, we hear about the confusing, stressful, insensitive, and manipulative marketplace in which customers feel trapped and victimized. American companies seem happy to be learning more and more about their customers every day. Yet customers are not the least bit appreciative.

Customers have learned to simply deal with it. They have become numb to the standard ways in which products and services are sold and delivered. They reluctantly tolerate sales clerks who mistreat them every time they buy a roll of film. They tirelessly work their way through the seemingly endless shelves of "new and improved" products at the grocery store. They continuously wade through the constant flow of mail offering them participation in reward programs. Simply put, the American consumer is fed up and wants a way out.

Most American businesses have been terribly slow in accepting this reality. For years, U.S. luxury carmakers surveyed customers, asking such questions as, "How satisfied are you with the cleanliness of our service department?" and "How was the free coffee in our waiting lounge?" The vast majority of consumers said they were highly satisfied. Yet when given an alternative product to purchase, many of these same "highly satisfied customers" traded in their Cadillac or Lincoln for a Lexus or Infinity. The surveys had captured customers' satisfaction levels but not the importance of the items being surveyed.[1]

Forcing a reanalysis of the conventional wisdom can lead to new discoveries in the marketplace. For most industries, the definition of *customer* is centered around the target customer. In most cases, it is a single buyer group. The pharmaceutical industry focuses almost exclusively on doctors. The clothing industry converges primarily on users; the office equipment industry on corporate purchasing departments.

However, there is normally a chain of customers who are directly or indirectly involved in the buying decision. The *purchasers* who pay for the product or service may differ from the actual *users,* who may be quite separated from the *influencers.* Each one of these groups may not value the same things. A purchasing agent may be more concerned with costs than the corporate user, who is far more interested in the ease of use. Similarly, a retailer may highly value a manufacturer's inventory program and creative financing. But consumer purchasers, although influenced by the entire process, would not value such things.

Bloomberg

In little over a decade, Bloomberg has become one of the largest and most profitable business information providers in the world. For years, the market was dominated by Reuters and Telerate. Focus was on the purchasers of the services, who valued standardized systems that made their life easier.

Bloomberg saw the conventional wisdom of the industry was backward. It was the trader and the analyst who made or lost millions of dollars a day for their employer. The premium customer of the service was not the information technology (IT) manager but the trader and analyst. So Bloomberg designed a system specifically to offer traders better value, one with easy-to-use terminals and keyboards labeled with familiar financial terms.[2]

Further, by focusing on the highest needs of its premium customer, Bloomberg saw another opportunity to lead the field. Traders and analysts make a lot of money but do not have a lot of time. Bloomberg decided to add information and purchasing services aimed at enhancing the user's personal life. Traders and analysts can buy flowers, clothing, and jewelry; make travel plans; visit the library; or shop for a new car—all at their desk.

By focusing on users rather than purchasers, Bloomberg created value that allows it to lead the field.

BUILDING AN ADVISORY BOARD

A customer-focused strategy for all buying groups is best found by creating an advisory board. In all cases, the quality of members of an advisory board will dictate the quality of focus. In addition, the quality of inquiry within the advisory board will directly influence the focus as well.

An effective advisory board should consist of premium customers, high-end vacillating customers, and potential customers.

As discussed in Chapter 1, premium customers are marked by four characteristics surrounding you, your product, or service:

1. The premium customer has a high need for your product.
2. The premium customer has a unique value need for your product.
3. The premium customer has a frequent need for your product.
4. The premium customer is an influencer of others.

The second group that should be represented in a strong advisory board is made up of customers at the high end of the vacillating group. As discussed in the paradigm of commodity value, the majority of your customers lie within the vacillating category. They are lost and confused. They want to be educated. They want to be treated like a doctor, not a patient.

Within the vacillating category, some customers are more lost and confused than others. Those vacillating customers, who are the best able to be educated and can most easily be moved into the premium category, should sit on your advisory board. These customers need to be asked the following questions: What are you doing now that I could be doing for you? What changes do you want to have help in dealing with? What long-term needs do you have? Once the answers are discovered, you can then formulate strategies to increase your value to them and bring them into the premium category.

Potential customers are the third group that should be represented on your advisory board. These are customers who have the ability to be your premium customers but are currently doing business with someone else. In order to lead the field, it is critical to constantly add new premium customers. Further, by seeking the counsel of potential customers, it is easier to keep one's pulse on shifts within the marketplace.

Whatever the size of the organization, well-structured advisory boards will successfully navigate you through the inevitable minefields of the marketplace.

Quicken

Innumerable examples exist of companies that have created effectual advisory boards and learned what the one thing of significance —what they did best—was to their premium customer. The company that revolutionized the way individuals and small businesses manage their finances saw their greatest competitor was not in the industry. As Intuit founder Scott Cook recalls, "The greatest competitor was the pencil. The pencil is a really tough and resilient substitute. Yet the entire industry had overlooked it."[3]

By simply asking potential buyers of Quicken software why they preferred a pencil to the computerized solutions, Intuit gained two critical insights: the pencil was much cheaper and much easier to use.

Intuit focused on bringing out both the decisive advantages that the computer has over the pencil—speed and accuracy—and the decisive advantages that the pencil has over computers— simplicity of use and low price—and eliminated everything else. With its user-friendly screen that replicates the user's own checkbook, Quicken is almost as simple to use as the pencil. Further, Intuit deleted all of the sophisticated features that were part of the industry's conventional wisdom and offered only a few basic functions most customers use. Simplifying the software cut costs. The end result was a breakthrough value created by Quicken and a re-creation of the industry—led by Intuit.

Fidelity Investments

Fidelity learned through an advisory board of current and potential customers that their highest need was easy access to information. It was quite possible for an individual investor to look up his or her stocks or mutual funds in the daily newspaper, but the process was not enjoyable. The newsprint was small and rubbed off on the reader's hands and clothes.

Fidelity developed a strategy to provide ideal electronic access to its products and services. Customers were able to personalize their experience with Fidelity's Web page and retrieve all of the information they wanted in a simple and clean manner. Fidelity is leading the personal finance industry by making easy-to-access information the value proposition rather than the products, services, and information themselves.[4]

Burger King

There are also an equal number of companies that have neglected to consult their advisory boards and plowed headstrong into a quagmire. In the late 1980s, Burger King slid into the doldrums because it lost focus on what it was doing right. The Herb the Nerd advertising campaign, highly publicized fights with franchisees, and menu diversification into pizza and seafood all knocked Burger King off its once high perch.

About five years ago, the focus was reshifted to address the highest need of Burger King's premium customer—quality product. Advertising was turned back to actually showing a Whopper on the grill and stressing the brand's core foods. In 1993, 27 menu items were eliminated. The end result has been a surge in sales in the United States and greater market share.

General Motors

General Motors also failed to listen to its advisory board about its Saturn division. Recent events have plagued the automaker. Annual summer strikes and foreign market slowdowns have both complicated the massive reorganization embarked on in 1995. Market share for the auto giant is falling in the United States, and management openly wonders if any of today's teenagers will ever consider buying a GM car. Throughout this turbulence, Saturn has been GM's shining star. As many say, the last best hope for GM in the U.S. market.

Since its introduction in 1990, Saturn has met the highest need of many of GM's premium customers. Saturn's customer-focused strategy has been brilliantly received by the marketplace, especially by younger consumers. However, almost since the beginning, both Saturn dealers and consumers have been begging for a full-size sedan and minivan. General Motors considered the issue superfluous and let the idea die on the vine. As a result, dealers and consumers were forced to look somewhere else. Saturn is finally slated to get a compact sedan in mid-2000 to late 2000, but many critics say it may be too little, too late.[5] GM may very well have missed the boat.

Pollo Tropical Restaurants

Larry J. Harris was only 27 when he opened his first Pollo Tropical restaurant in 1988. Located in the heart of Little Havana in Miami's Cuban district, Pollo Tropical catered to the Latin taste of chicken marinated in *mojo* basting. Coupled with a charming Spanish-style architecture, Pollo Tropical was an instant hit in Latino-dominated Miami.[6]

By 1993, Harris had opened seven more restaurants in Miami and in October of that year went public, earning $24 million from the initial public offering (IPO). The money from Wall Street was put into opening more stores—this time outside of the Miami area. Pollo Tropical restaurants in Chicago, Long Island, Tampa, and St. Petersburg all opened in 1994. Harris was named Ernst & Young's 1995 Florida Entrepreneur of the Year.

However, almost overnight, things began to fall apart. The new stores outside of Miami closed almost immediately after they opened. It seemed northerners were not at all responsive to the distinctive Latin cuisine of Pollo Tropical. What happened to Pollo Tropical is the same thing that happens to thousands of successful, new start-ups every year. In the case of Pollo Tropical, the highest need of the premium customer was to eat genuine Latin-style chicken in a typical Latin environment. This was most appealing to Latinos, not northerners, who preferred Boston Market and Kentucky Fried Chicken.

By not focusing on the highest need of its premium customers, Pollo Tropical was unable to lead a field that it probably should have. Today, Pollo Tropical is getting back on track. Franchises are opening in Santo Domingo, Quito, and São Paulo: places where its distinctive style will be met with open arms by its premium customers—Latinos.

BRANDING YOURSELF, YOUR PRODUCT, OR YOUR SERVICE

After discovering the optimal customer-focused strategy, it is critical to brand your product or service accordingly. Creating a successful brand is critical in achieving the market dominance necessary for attaining full price. It is necessary to build a significant image around the one thing you do best. Brands are all around us. They dominate the landscape and invariably lead the field.

The creation of a strong, dominant brand is rooted in three steps: owning terminology; defining the terminology; and putting the terminology on everything you have.

Owning terminology is the effective use of words that reflects the highest needs of your premium customer. Having already learned what the highest needs are through the advisory board, it is now possible to build a brand around those needs.

Individuals do not typically think of themselves as a brand. Nevertheless, the leaders in a particular field are more often than not associated with terminology they claim as their own.

Even though there are thousands of outstanding management consultants throughout the nation, only Tom Peters is associated with "excellence." While he was alive, Joe DiMaggio would not sign any agreement to appear in public unless he was introduced as "The Greatest Living Ballplayer." Ted Williams and Willie Mays may have disagreed. Yet it was DiMaggio who had the brand around him—not Williams or Mays.

Once a brand is established around the highest need of the premium customer, it needs to be defined accordingly. Hy-Vee, the grocery store chain, is "A Helpful Smile in Every Aisle." If you visit a Hy-Vee store, you know this to be true. A customer is warmly greeted by everyone with a smile and a desire to make your experience as comfortable as possible.

Finally, once the terminology is defined, it needs to be put everywhere. The next time you go to Wal-Mart, count the number of places where you see "We sell for less." I assure you it will be well over 100 places.

Cisco Systems

In the mid-1980s, the management of Cisco Systems saw the greatest threat to the future of computer networking to be the slow data exchange rate. At the same time, demand was exploding as the number of Internet users was doubling every 100 days, so Cisco could clearly see the problem would eventually worsen.

To best respond to the coming crisis, Cisco decided to focus exclusively on routers, switches, and other networking devices that created breakthrough value for customers. By offering fast data exchanges in a seamless networking environment, Cisco met the highest need of the networked customer. Its insight was as much about value innovation as it is about technology.[7] Innovation became Cisco's brand.

Today, more than 80 percent of all Internet traffic flows through Cisco's products, and its margins are in the 60 percent range. Through creating value by responding to its premium customer's highest need, Cisco Systems leads the field.

Champion Enterprises

For years, Michigan-based Champion Enterprises was one of the largest manufacturers of prefabricated housing in the country. Unfortunately, the company almost always lost money. The image of prefabricated housing was generally low because it was dismally standardized and projected an image of low quality. The vast majority of industry customers were poor and rural.

After nearly going bankrupt in 1992, the new CEO of Champion asked his management a simple question: What business are we in? It was decided that the past would no longer provide any answers, so a new focus was sought.

Champion decided its potential premium customers were not the rural buyer but the lower-to-middle-income consumer who is either buying or renting an apartment. Champion decided to allow these potential buyers to choose such high-end options as fireplaces, skylights, and even vaulted ceilings—actually, customizing their own home. Customizing removed the stigma of a prefabricated home. By stressing the flexibility in design *and* the lower economies of scale, far more people have become interested in purchasing a prefabricated home. In short, Champion has changed the definition of prefabricated housing, created a brand, and now leads the field.[8]

Kevin Brown

One of the most debated questions among baseball fans is: If you had to win just one game, which pitcher would you want on the mound? The most common responses are Roger Clemens, Greg Maddux, and Randy Johnson. Everyone would agree any of them would put your team in a strong position to win *the* game.

However, when baseball executives throughout the major leagues are asked the same question, they almost unanimously agree that Kevin Brown would be the best choice. Brown is not a hard thrower like Clemens or Johnson. He does not have the pinpoint accuracy of Maddux. Unlike the other three, Brown is not a shoo-in for the Hall of Fame. Brown has never won a Cy Young award and his career numbers pale next to the others. Yet he has the "stuff," as baseball insiders call it, to overcome all of the hysteria and win the big game like nobody else.

In the free-agent market following the 1998 season, Clemens, Johnson, and Brown were all seeking new deals with new teams.

Although Clemens and Johnson each accepted seven-digit deals, it was Brown who received the largest contract in baseball history—more than $105 million over seven years from the Los Angeles Dodgers. Baseball experts attributed Brown's deal to one thing—his ability to be counted on in the big game. For baseball owners, there is nothing more critical to the success of their organization. Kevin Brown understood this, branded himself accordingly, and achieved full price for himself.

Within particular brands, there also exist subbrands. Hy-Vee, the grocery store chain, also has restaurants on its premises that are called Kitchens. As a result, while shopping at a Hy-Vee, a customer receives "a smile in every aisle" with the opportunity to eat lunch in the Kitchen. The creation of a friendly, cozy environment makes Hy-Vee a leader in the cutthroat grocery store market.

Another successful subbrand has been the Mr. Goodwrench campaign of General Motors. Through the establishment of Mr. Goodwrench as a subbrand of the vehicles it produces, General Motors created a complete package for the customer. Buyers knew they were receiving not only the quality of a General Motors car but also the integrity of the best-trained mechanics in the world.

Hyde Park Jewelers

Hyde Park Jewelers in Denver, Colorado, a three-outlet jewelry chain, may not be a household name, but it is nevertheless the leader in its class. In the early 1970s, Steven Rosdal, weary of the rat race on Wall Street, fled New York to seek a better life in Albuquerque, New Mexico. He made his living trading with American Indians on the Navajo and Hopi reservations for turquoise and silver jewelry that he would sell to retailers across the country. His customers included Nordstrom, Macy's, and Saks.

Michael Pollak, at the time a University of Denver junior majoring in retail marketing, began purchasing craft jewelry from Rosdal and selling it in a shop on campus. After Pollak's graduation in

1972, he teamed up with Rosdal to found a silver manufacturing company in Albuquerque.

The company did well for three years, but then things began to change. The market had become oversupplied, and American Indian craft jewelry was beginning to fade from fashion. Sensing a need for a change in course, Rosdal and Pollak opened the first Hyde Park fine jewelry store at a 1,200-square-foot location in Denver.

Since then, Hyde Park stores have been added in Las Vegas and Aspen. And in early 1999, the flagship Denver store graduated to a 10,000-square-foot spot in the upscale Cherry Creek Shopping Center. Instead of American Indian craft jewelry, the stores now deal in fine jewelry, gemstones, and prestigious brand timepieces, such as Rolex, Pasquale Bruni, Gucci, and Breuning.

Pollak and Rosdal have succeeded in the fine jewelry business because they saw a demand that was not being met. Says Rosdal, "We work in a retailing sector in which the consumer has a lot of threshold resistance. We try to help the customer make the decision by providing an environment that's upscale without being intimidating."

Hyde Park does that by incorporating customer intimacy into its corporate culture. The chain has a workforce of 60, all well versed in the art of fine jewelry. However, snobs need not apply. "So much depends on the relationship with the client," Rosdal continues. "We try to encourage the client to look at us as their peers." The customer experience is enhanced by value-added services throughout the store. Clients in the market for custom-made jewelry will be able to visualize and help design their purchases with the aid of a computer-aided design (CAD) program that allows an image of the piece to be rotated and manipulated on-screen. If the client wishes to base a new work on an existing piece of jewelry, the latter can be scanned into the CAD program with a 3-D camera.

In addition, each store sports an Interactive Media and Learning Center consisting of a comfortable couch and multimedia touchscreen unit that provides pertinent information in such areas as jewels, gemology, and watches. It also functions as television. "Perfect for husbands who want to check out the football game while the wife designs her new earrings," quips Pollak.[9]

BENCHMARKING YOUR PROCESS

The third strategy leaders use to lead the field is benchmarking their process. A dominant leader is able to define at what level it is able to deliver something consistently. Then the level is quantified. For years, Domino's Pizza led the field by benchmarking its process: "30 minutes or less." UPS did the same with "overnight delivery."

The critical factors in benchmarking your process are making it tangible and important to the customer. Doing so creates value and leads to full price.

NationsBank

NationsBank consistently leads the field of personal banking by implementing a customer-defined vision of ideal interactions with the bank via telebanking.[10] Customers have defined their highest need as acquiring the most relevant information—in either a live or automated format—in an easy manner.

NationsBank set up a program in which information is easily accessible to their customer service representatives (CSRs). Further, training was provided to enhance the performance of the CSRs. The ultimate goal was to benchmark the process through which the service is delivered instead of focusing on the products or services themselves.

MasterCard

When MasterCard wanted to get an outside-in view of what its customers value during interactions with its telephone call centers, it found that many customers who have dealings with call centers subsequently rated responsive service as more important than interest rates. Today, MasterCard uses a call-center strategy that has been defined by its customers and integrated with its own internal operation. Such a process provides MasterCard with the capability to align itself with what its premium customers value most.[11]

Some leaders benchmark their process and create value by getting rid of hassles for their customers.

Dyson Vacuum Cleaners

One of the most profitable vacuum cleaner manufacturers in the world, Dyson learned early on the most important concern for the user was buying and changing the bag. Its premium customers told it there was nothing more trying on their patience than changing a bag full of dust, animal hair, and the like in the room that was just cleaned. As a result, Dyson designed its vacuum cleaners to obliterate the costly and annoying activities of buying and changing the bag. Through the process of elimination, Dyson benchmarked itself.[12]

Shred-It

According to the studies conducted by Shred-It, a Canadian-based paper-shredding company, 70 percent of companies shredded their paperwork with small (and sometimes dangerous) office shredders that could do half a pound of paper per minute. The management of Shred-It identified technologies that allowed documents to be destroyed 40 times faster than traditional office shredders and thereby shifted liability from the client to Shred-It.

In benchmarking its process, Shred-It offered its customers a 40–1 productivity differential. Its first major client, a General Electric plant outside Toronto, figured it was paying secretaries $33 for every 100 pounds of paper shredded. The management of Shred-It offered its 40–1 differential and chopped up 400 pounds for $13.[13]

Today, Shred-It has established 32 franchises, most of them in the United States, and operates a fleet of 34 mobile shredders in Ontario. It is increasingly known throughout the industry as the 40–1 company.

SUMMARY

To lead the field in your particular industry, it is critical to attach yourself to your customers while keeping an eye on your competition. To identify the one thing that sets them apart from everyone else in the eyes of their premium customers, leading companies do the following:

- Build an advisory board

- Brand themselves, their product, or service

- Benchmark their process

CHAPTER 3

Selling the Program

"The creation of value is not about increasing your customer's satisfaction. It is about taking responsibility for your customer's results."

—Thom Winninger

The world is full of information and experts that instruct businesses on how to build customer loyalty. The conventional wisdom throughout industry today seems to encourage companies to study, evaluate, or implement strategies aimed at cultivating strong relationships with their best customers.

Concepts like "customer focus" and "customer satisfaction" are warmly embraced. Most companies have things to sell, and they sell these things to customers. Who isn't focusing on satisfying customers?

However, satisfaction and focus simply aren't enough. If you are going to be a leader in your markets, you are going to have to learn new words like *intimacy, interaction, loyalty,* and, perhaps more important, *strategic alliance.*[1] Strategic alliance is a single-thread relationship. It is being one. Such a relationship is built on a mutually agreed-to plan that reflects the nature and needs of the parties involved. This is not a rewording of old terminology or a redefining of the same, tired concepts of "sales and service." Instead, it is a paradigm shift, moving away from satisfaction and toward loyalty.

The constant push to offer customers the greatest possible value for their product is inevitably leading companies into close partnerships that go far beyond discrete sales. Successful companies and individuals are becoming intimately involved in the day-to-day operations of their customers' businesses. Leaders are constantly building and improving the ability of their customers to better themselves.

The leaders in their industry focus on the program, process, or system that surrounds their product or service—not the product or service itself. A leader sells a program that helps customers make money or their life easier. By encompassing their product or service around their processes, leaders are able to maximize the value of their product and achieve full price.

Almost every product sold is intimately tied to several aspects of a process—that is, production, conversion, technology, logistics, distribution. The more a company learns about its customers' buying process, the more it can customize programs and systems to assist customers in becoming part of that process. In short, the more a company helps the customer, the stronger the relationship becomes. The end result is a product or service that becomes so critical to customers that they are willing to base their future on it. Pressure is taken off price, which becomes an ancillary issue.

The key to building this invaluable relationship with your customers is centered around the selling of the program, process, or system to which your product is most intricately linked. The emergence of thematic dining motifs provides insight into the strength of selling the program or process rather than the product itself. "Eatertainment" establishments like Hardrock Cafe, Dave & Buster's, and the Rainforest Cafe offer food and service that is no better than other restaurants that charge half the price. Their ability to command full price is centered around the themes and environment—aka the program—that surround the meal. By placing the focus on the program surrounding the food rather than the food itself, these eateries are able to create more value and therefore charge much higher menu prices for the same food.

FOCUSING ON WHAT THE PRODUCT OR SERVICE DOES, NOT WHAT IT IS

There are three ways in which leaders successfully sell the program. The first method is to focus on what the product or service actually does rather than merely what it is. In other words, concentrate on the benefits of the product instead of simply the product itself. The idea of selling the benefits instead of the product is proactive in nature. Salespeople might consider this to be just another in a long line of selling tactics. Focusing on what the product does is not merely another hammer in a salesperson's toolbox. It is much more than that. It is strategy built on new millennium thinking that runs contrary to the principles behind mass distribution and production.

Mass distributors have attempted to optimize product supply by forcing customers to come to them. A product is scattered throughout as many as outlets as possible with the hope that if we distribute it, they will come. Inventory is built in anticipation of potential, yet uncertain, demand. Forecasting and even guessing become the standard methods for building future business. Even if most companies can accurately forecast their future requirements, they will still fall short in knowing exactly which products will be needed at which locations and at what times.[2]

To properly sell the program and the benefits surrounding the product or service, the correct identification of its benefits is critical. For example, the Book-of-the-Month Club successfully focuses on a reading program rather than simply buying books.

The rise of personalized shopping and meal services throughout the United States reveals what can happen when the focus is taken off the product and placed on the benefits of the product. Thriving businesses all over the country not only deliver the product but also customize the delivery to the highest need of their customers.

Zany Brainy

In the world of children's toys, Toys "R" Us dominates more than one-third of the market. Its deep-discount pricing and huge aisles of selection make Toys "R" Us a dominant force. However, in an attempt to make the toy-shopping experience more customer oriented, Zany Brainy has been able to successfully set itself apart. The management of the Philadelphia-based chain found a latent demand on the part of children and parents concerning the way toys are sold. Zany Brainy is not simply a toy store; it is a multimedia educational experience.

The majority of a store's staff—called Kidsultants—are retired teachers and learning specialists trained to offer insights and advice on selecting products. There is a constant slate of events, such as readings, crafts workshops, and fundraising events—all of which cement the store as a family-fun destination. Sections of the store are marked Discovery, Creativity, or Young Builders and are grouped further by such divisions as product category (rocks and minerals) or age group. The store carries nothing violent, sexist, or toxic; and books, software, and CD-ROMs play a heavy part in the merchandise mix.[3]

The ability of Zany Brainy to make the process of buying toys a family-centered activity rather than just another walk through the aisles creates value for its stores.

Mobile Psychological Services

Mobile Psychological Service (MPS) is a wonderful example of how focusing on the benefits can maximize the value of a product or service. The hectic pace and awful congestion in Manhattan can grate on even the most laid-back individual. For high-strung, type A personalities, life in the Big Apple can be downright traumatic.

New York leads the nation in the number of visits to therapists per capita. However, it is estimated that one in four appointments in New York are canceled as a result of sudden schedule changes or traffic jams. To alleviate the problem, MPS decided to take the couch to the people. Ursula Strauss, cofounder of MPS, recognized the existence of a clientele that couldn't come to therapy on a regular basis but still needed help with things like substance abuse and balancing work with personal life.

When clients feel the need for counseling, they call a dispatch center that sends a licensed therapist in a mobile office to their door. The client enters the van, which is centered around a plump couch and decorated in drapes and blinds over darkened windows.

A session with MPS is well over the average hourly rate for therapists, with a $50 charge added if the patient wants a ride to another destination. The fleet of vehicles has grown exponentially and franchising is in the works for other major metropolitan areas throughout the country.

Through the integration of its service with the lifestyle of its clients, MPS has been better able to create maximum value for its services.

America Online

The explosion of local, regional, and national Internet service providers (ISPs) has compelled industry leader America Online (AOL) to remain focused on the program it offers the marketplace. The plethora of companies fighting for the new Internet customer makes this one of the fiercest markets in the country today. Except for a few exceptions, almost all ISPs offer the same services, so it is becoming increasingly more difficult to create value and set oneself apart.

America Online's success from the beginning has been its ability to provide an interactive experience that is easy, useful, fun, and affordable with access to unique brand content as well as to the Internet. The process of going online is much more than simply surfing the Web. By introducing new versions of its service to highlight more of its proprietary information, AOL provides its customers with a wider array of benefits. Doing so makes the AOL experience more rewarding and valuable.

The Ritz-Carlton Hotel Company

Ritz-Carlton hotels observe the preferences of each guest during the guest's stay—pillow type, radio stations, and midnight snacks. The information is stored in a database and used to tailor the service customers receive on their next visit. The more times a customer stays at a Ritz-Carlton hotel, the more the company knows and the better the experience is for the guest. Ritz-Carlton can truthfully claim your stay is not in merely another hotel room but is your "home away from home."

EMPHASIZING THE WAY THE PRODUCT OR SERVICE IS BOUGHT OR SOLD

Beyond stressing what the product does, the second manner in which leaders sell the program is by focusing on the ways in which the product or service is bought or sold.

Dear to the hearts of consumers today is the ability to use credit cards. Because of the convenience that comes with buying with a credit card, millions and millions of consumers have access to more products and services than ever before. Huge revolving balances notwithstanding, Americans are increasingly shopping with only their credit cards. It is safer and easier than using cash. Go out for dinner on a Friday night and count how many people pay with a credit card; it will probably be nearly everyone in the restaurant. The proliferation of credit cards has led to greater emphasis on how products and services are bought and sold. The process of the transaction is, in many cases, becoming more important than the product or service itself.

Further, market research shows a rapidly increasing number of car buyers who first look at the lease options and then the vehicle. Leasing has become so prevalent that dealers now structure much of their advertising and promotions around the lease itself. The next time you pick up a newspaper or watch television, count the number of car advertisements that focus exclusively on a leasing program. The emphasis on leasing further illustrates the importance of the process of buying or selling.

The multi-billion-dollar time-share industry is centered on the proposition that the investment in a weekly vacation is of a higher value than purchasing a vacation home. The flexibility and ease in purchasing a time-share is what gives it value.

Interclean

Interclean, a leading maintenance supply distributor, was concerned that it was selling more but earning less. After establishing an advisory board, management learned the highest need of premium customers was not lower pricing but peace of mind. The customers were always fearful they might not have all of the products they needed in an emergency situation.

The focus of the company was therefore shifted from merely the sales and service of the product to a comprehensive inventory control program ensuring that the products are on the shelf when the maintenance specialist needs them. The sale of a complete management inventory system—including all of the maintenance products—provided security to customers from knowing they will never run out of something.

ChemStation

A similar case is ChemStation. The Dayton, Ohio, manufacturer of industrial soap for such uses as car washes and cleaning factory floors, sells a product that is typically viewed as a commodity. ChemStation realized long ago its survival and success were directly related to building a program around the buying of its product. After independently analyzing each customer's needs, ChemStation custom-formulates the right mixture of soap, which goes into a standard ChemStation tank on the customer's premises. Through regular monitoring, the company learns each customer's usage pattern and presciently delivers more soap before the customer has to ask for it. This practice eliminates the need for customers to spend time creating or reviewing orders. They don't know which soap formulation they have, how much is in inventory, or when it was delivered. They only know—and care—that the soap works and is always there when they need it.[4]

Xerox

Xerox Corporation provides us with another strong example of how to integrate a product with the purchase process. Rather than looking just at copying machines and printers, Xerox focuses on the basic concept of the document and document management. While much of Xerox's sales are still one-time hardware purchases, Xerox has been focusing in on identifying and streamlining customers' processes for the exchange of hard copy and electronic documents.

Xerox offers its premium customers the management of all document production and distribution through carefully scheduled digital printing technology. Xerox employees enter a customer's business and assess how they can make things better by using Xerox products. Doing so invariably reduces redundancies, speeds delivery, and improves accuracy in billing, accounting, and other document-intensive operations. The end result is a program that has a high value to Xerox customers.

Sealed Air

Sealed Air is a Saddle Brook, New Jersey, manufacturer, of packaging products like Styrofoam and bubble wrap. For years, the firm has been dedicated to making their customers' immediate needs match Sealed Air's long-term objectives. Realizing the growing need for customized attention, Sealed Air developed the Instapak System, a custom-designed process for on-site packaging that integrates the customers' manufacturing and distribution processes. Now used by such nationally known companies as NordicTrack and Waterford Wedgewood, the Instapak System is now being taught at its customers' in-house marketing meetings and training sessions throughout the country.[5] The Instapak System has become a vital element in the future of Sealed Air's customers.

USAA

Although the U.S. military's downsizing dramatically hurt the profits of companies catering to service personnel and their families, USAA has sailed through the 1990s with double-digit growth.

United States Automobile Association began as an auto insurer for highly mobile military officers. Because auto insurance is regulated at the state level, moving between states normally requires canceling an existing policy and applying for a new one—a time-consuming process for a time-constrained officer. In order to best attend to the needs of their customers, USAA became a licensed property and casualty insurer in every state to allow its policyholders to change their policies with a single phone call.[6]

USAA's value is created by making the policy-buying process so simple that military officers would not even consider changing insurers regardless of the price of the insurance. Today, USAA has captured more than 90 percent of all active-duty officers.

Help in the Buying Process from the Internet

The Internet has become a massive experimental laboratory for new technologies intended to make the buying process easier. Every year a larger percentage of Americans have threatened to avoid the frantic shopping malls and do their Christmas shopping over the Web. New technologies, which include three-dimensional graphics, interactive customer service using text and voice, improved search engines, and automated shopping agents called "bots" (for robots), are among many of the ways merchants are trying to capture the interest of shoppers.

SharperImage.com. Shoppers on the Internet are obviously unable to pick up an item and examine it, but they can still approximate the experience. The Sharper Image <www.sharperimage.com> has a 3-D-enhanced catalog online that enables customers to view images in three dimensions. Digitized images of many products can be rotated just by clicking and dragging with the mouse, allowing viewing from any angle. The user can even manipulate the object to see how the lid opens or how it folds for storage.

Landsend.com. Lands' End <www.landsend.com> allows a woman to create a personal model on the screen that approximates her physical characteristics. Once the model's dimensions, hairstyle, and skin color are established, the shopper can send the model into a virtual dressing room to try on clothes from the catalog. The model can be rotated to show how the clothes look from all angles while the colors can be changed with a simple mouse-click.[7]

Furniture.com. This Web site is enabling shoppers to arrange and rearrange room layouts on their computer screens, to see whether a particular sofa will fit in the living room, or whether a new chair will clash with the fabric on the old chairs. The company will even send fabric swatches through the mail.[8]

Gateway.com. Kenneth Stickevers, vice president of Gateway. com (the Internet division of computer maker Gateway), says the ability to track orders lured customers to visit the Gateway Web site. "A person will check on the status of an order five times over the two-week period it takes for the computer to arrive as opposed to one phone call during the same period before the Web," he said.[9]

Integrated customer service is the philosophy at Gateway where, Stickevers said, a customer should be able to get the same level of service on the Web, on the phone, or in the company's stores. He adds, "The only reason to be on the Net is customer service and building relationships with your customers. A company should do everything to make customer service and the buying process as simple as possible for shoppers." He concludes by saying with the creation of the Web, "There are so many opportunities for companies to serve customers and their bottom line."[10]

Nordstrom.com. Once customers send a query to Nordstrom.com for something they cannot find in the site's electronic catalog, a member of Nordstrom's personal shoppers Web team will hunt down the product and send back news of the price, color, sizes, specifications, and so on. These personal shoppers work at selected stores and deal only with e-mail requests. They will follow up to customers either by e-mail or a phone call. "Our goal is to provide our customers with a shopping experience that's on their terms," says Colleen Chapman, the Internet marketing director of Nordstrom.com.[11]

RECOGNIZING THE IMPORTANCE OF WHAT IS DONE AFTER THE SALE

The third technique for selling the program stresses doing something after the sale. One night last August, my old gas grill cooked its last hamburger. As a result, my wife decided to surprise me with a new grill for my birthday.

The following morning she set out to a discount center to buy my birthday gift. Because of the vast selection and low prices advertised, as well as the fact that my wife is an ardent coupon clipper, it seemed only logical she would begin her journey there. It didn't go very well. The young associate, whom she eventually tracked down after ten minutes of wandering aimlessly, wasn't the best man for the job. Never asking what she wanted, he pointed out the two grills on the floor, which were not at all what she had in mind. He suggested there might be some others on top of the shelving. After they both had climbed up the ladder, my wife scanned the dusty inventory the best she could and decided on one particular model. Then, she proceeded to help lower down the 120-pound box. Once they were back on terra firma again, she inquired if they could deliver the grill fully assembled. He looked at her in shock. His only response was to say my wife could park in their loading dock while she loaded the box into the car herself. Despite the great difficulties, my wife, the ardent saver, decided to buy a grill there. After waiting another 20 minutes in the checkout line, she finally headed home with my birthday gift.

On unwrapping the package on my birthday, my heart dropped when I realized assembly was required. I knew it would take me at least a week to put it together. So as not to congest my garage and alienate my loving wife, I spent the next several days assembling the grill in my den. When I finally had it almost all together, I discovered the wheels were missing. I immediately called the discount center and, after waiting on hold for nearly an hour, tracked down the associate who originally sold the grill to my wife. He told me that the store has no wheels or spare parts of any kind for the grill. His only suggestion was to tell me to bring the entire unit back to the store so we could make an exchange. I informed him I cannot move the unit without the wheels. Uninterested in my dilemma, he flippantly told me to call a store that might have the wheels. And then he hung up.

Disgusted with what was happening, I jumped in my car and headed to the corner hardware store in search of the wheels. When I entered the store, the first thing I saw was a beautiful grill with a small sign hanging above it that read, "We assemble and deliver all grills." Moreover, the price was only $35 more than the price my wife paid the discount center!

When the salesperson at the hardware store approached me, I eagerly asked him if it was true that the store would actually assemble and deliver the grill to my home. When he said yes, I happily pulled out my credit card and told him I wanted that same model sent to my home that same day along with the extra set of wheels. He responded, "No problem." Later that day, I had two new grills on my back deck and was able to cook four dozen hamburgers at the same time.

Like the grill store, leading companies are learning to stress what happens after the sale. Free assembly and delivery are becoming ways to increase the value of products in these fast-paced times. As the father of four still at home, the ugliest words I have ever heard at the holidays are "some assembly required." I cannot tell you the number of Christmas Eves I have stayed up trying to put together a foosball table or a Barbie dollhouse.

Leaders who provide these services allow customers to dedicate their time to more important aspects of their life, such as family and friends—and sleep! Service programs for cars, trucks, SUVs, motorcycles, and power equipment assure buyers of dependable use for the product. Better warranty programs allow the product to have longer, productive usage. Each of these creates the needed value we all seek for our products and services.

Merck-Medco

Many senior citizens now obtain their prescriptions from Merck-Medco, a mail-order pharmacy. Medco maintains extensive patient databases to monitor the medical histories and prescription usage of customers over time. Retirees have their orders sent directly to their doctor's office. In addition, customers are sent an automatic reminder to refill their prescriptions. At the same time, Medco monitors a customer's therapies to guard against possibly harmful drug interactions. To address any concerns customers may have about side effects after taking a medication, a 24-hour call center is staffed by pharmacists to answer questions or offer advice about how to properly take the medication.[12]

L.L. Bean

L.L. Bean maintains a 24-hour call center to help customers replace a lost article of clothing they may have purchased ten years ago. For example, a customer calls about a jacket purchased by his wife for his birthday when they were living in another city. In a matter of minutes, the sales agent identifies the old jacket, locates a replacement model in the current catalog, suggests a matching size and color, and orders the jacket. The replacement jacket arrives three days later.[13]

Snap-on Inc.

Snap-on Inc. has for more than 75 years built a business model primarily as a toolmaker that combines the top-drawer cachet of a Louis Vuitton, the credit philosophy of a Wells Fargo, and the convenience of the Good Humor man. Based in Kenosha, Wisconsin, Snap-on has viewed its well-oiled delivery system and fleet of technical representatives as two elements of its success. To sell its wares, Snap-on's 5,700 franchise dealers and sales representatives steer their easily spotted white vans to more than 350,000 automobile dealerships, service stations, and independent garages around the United States.

Well before the competition realized it, Snap-on understood that its main customer, the successful independent garage owner, was an astute businessperson. To the garage owner, time was money, and if he could get the right tools without having to leave work to buy them, he would gladly pay a higher price and become a regular customer.[14]

As the demand for high-technology tools such as diagnostic systems for on-board computers grew, Snap-on quickly recognized it would also have to provide technical support as well as the excellent service it was already known for. For Snap-on, this has been a simple and powerful transformation. Says Martin Silverman, a partner in the Chicago office of Booz Allen & Hamilton, "You don't sell diagnostic systems and software the same way you sell hand tools. This is not about the feel of the tool in your hand, or the fit and finish. It's about functionality, and it has required the field force to get an understanding of a different kind of tool."[15] Fortunately for Snap-on and, more important, for its customers, this transformation to high technology has become as seamless as hammering a nail or tightening a screw.

SUMMARY

The leaders in their industry focus on the program, process, or system that surrounds their product or service —not on the product or service itself. A leader sells a program that helps the customer make money. By encompassing their product or service around their processes, leaders are able to maximize the value of their product and achieve full price.

In selling the program, leaders often implement one or a combination of three strategies:

- Focusing on what the product does, not what it is

- Emphasizing the way the product is bought or sold

- Recognizing the importance of what is done after the sale

CHAPTER 4

Vertical Integration

"The successful company focuses on how to best provide value for its customers, not on how to beat its competitors."

—Thom Winninger

Today's customer-dominated marketplace is doing all that it can to offer the best possible choices to consumers. With more companies than ever before competing for the customer's business, it is critical to create an environment in which consumers feel as though they have complete control at their disposal.

Choice is a fundamental tenet of our political and economic systems. You have the choice to vote for candidate X or Y, or even Z as well. You can also choose not to vote at all. You can decide which skill level you want to attain in your field—dramatically influencing your future compensation. You can stay in bed or get up and go to work. It's your choice.

In the new economy, the choices available to the consumer are greater than ever before. However, customers have less and less time for making choices. Customers are screaming out for the opportunity to purchase products and services that come together.

Concepts like "one-stop shopping" and "single-source supply" are dramatically changing the way you do business and your job. They come from customer need rather than advertising hype. The customer in the new economy is saying, "I'm busier today than ever before. There are an incredible amount of things competing for my limited time—work, family, personal development, traffic, significant others, mass media, recreation, and on and on. I want one place to buy all that I need, to make fewer decisions, to save time."

What a wonderful opportunity we have in front of us as we enter the 21st century! Customers want everything we can offer them. They want us to provide all the answers. And most important, if we do it right, they are willing to pay full price—no questions asked.

In light of this fantastic opportunity for the future, most businesses are still stuck in the a la carte mode—that is, providing the marketplace with only one choice at one price point. Occasionally accessories are offered and discount prices advertised; yet these fall far short of achieving the full potential for you, your product, or your service.

In my work with some of America's most successful companies, I have discovered the leaders in their industries are the ones who best provide the marketplace with clear, distinct, and complete choices. Leaders effectively design, manage, coordinate, and complete the entire package that is eventually sold. The imperative of *vertical integration* accomplishes this critical task. The following illustration may best illustrate the idea of integrating vertically.

I constantly remind my supermarket clients that there are two distinct ways to sell a turkey. At Thanksgiving and Christmas, Americans by the tens of millions flock to their local grocery store to purchase the turkey for their holiday meal. The vast majority of the turkeys available are warehoused in the freezer section. Customers line up around an ice-covered bin and throw prepackaged turkeys around until they find the one that is most appealing to them. In most stores, this annual ritual normally takes place next to unrelated products like bagels and frozen juice concentrate. In this scenario, the turkeys are sold alone—a la carte. They are disconnected from the other products that go along with the traditional meal and its preparation—gravy, stuffing, cranberry sauce, basters, and thermometers. This method of selling the turkey does nothing to the help the customer save time. Further, it disconnects the product. By not attending to the real need of the customer—convenience and time saving—the perceived value of the turkey is greatly diminished. It is reduced to a mere commodity, where the only real interest to the customer is the price per pound.

A much better way to get more money for the turkey is to connect the bird with products that can be integrated with it. Instead of putting the turkey in aisle 6, the stuffing in aisle 3, the cranberry sauce in aisle 8, and the cooking pan and bag in aisle 12, put them together. Create a one-stop center that offers several different packages of Holiday Meal Kits. Such choices for the customer are inherently value added. They are convenient and save time. They take the focus off the price per pound and bring full price ever closer.

There are three elements to vertical integration: (1) creating packages, (2) the "Magic of 3," and (3) valuating the choices.

CREATING PACKAGES

The ability to vertically integrate your product or service should be centered on the following proposition: What else can your customers buy that would make a particular product or service valuable to them? In other words, what can you connect your product or service to that makes it more complete? Or, more simply, how can you create packages?

Creating packages has to revolve around the needs of the customer. It cannot be emphasized enough that customers are seeking total solutions. As stated previously, they want one place to buy everything they need.

For products and services, the proliferation of telecommunications services provides a strong example of integrating all related products into a value-added package. It is widely held by many industry experts that both the business and the home of the future will have access to cable television, fixed and mobile telephones, Internet and online services, intranet services, data services, and number portability, all through a single cable. This single source for data and communication has led Bill Gates, the chairman of Microsoft, to conclude that the company that develops the software for this package will lead the field in the 21st century.

On a simpler level, the power of packaging can be seen at your corner hot dog stand. People will pay much more for a hot dog with chili or mustard than for a plain dog. They will also pay more for the same hot dog if it comes packaged with a can of soda and a bag of potato chips.

Oscar Mayer's Munchables are viable packages because they include not only the sandwich meat but also the cheese, crackers, and condiments. And Kellogg's has begun to connect its products by offering Breakfast Mates, which contain cereal, milk, and a spoon in a single refrigerator carton.

Brink's

Brink's Inc., the security company based in Irving, Texas, is integrating several aspects of its traditional service. Although millions of cash-based businesses have relied on Brink's to protect their money, research consistently showed that customers wanted more. To meet this growing demand for a comprehensive service, Brink's developed the CompuSafe Service—a computerized, single cash-handling system that integrates a CompuSafe unit, armored transportation, deposit processing, banking, and hardware/software maintenance into one service.[1]

Suparossa Pizza and Old Style Beer

Survey after survey reveals that the Midwest consumes nearly twice as much beer and pizza per capita as any other region in the United States. Recently, marketers of leading beer and pizza brands in the region integrated forces for an in-store grocery store meal of these two popular items. Old Style, the leading regional beer in the country, is the second-largest brand in the Chicago area. It has formed an alliance with Suparossa, the leading frozen pizza in the region. In-store displays are placed in the beer aisles of participating supermarkets in Chicago, including 170 Jewel/Osco stores; 70 Dominick's units; 70 Eagle locations; 18 Cub Foods stores; and 17 Omni stores.

Bob Perry, director of marketing at Biagio's Gourmet Foods, Suparossa's parent company, explains the success of the integration this way: "Customers do not have a lot of time, so selling the concept of a full meal in the supermarket makes sense. By effectively integrating with Old Style, we have been able to create a higher perceived value of our product. We are not merely another frozen pizza. We are the great midwestern meal."[2]

Sun Life of Canada

Sun Life of Canada has become the leader in retirement plan services to Canadian companies with up to 99 employees. Its integrated RQ-EZ program includes administration, recordkeeping, education support materials, and, of course, investments for their customers. The single-source supply focuses on small companies that have neither the staff nor the time to manage all aspects of their 401(k) plans and has resulted in a boon. Client after client praises Sun Life for integrating all of the key facets of retirement plan services into one.

GMZ Associates

GMZ Associates Ltd., a Chicago-based firm, has launched its Wet'N Brush, a toothbrush with toothpaste already in the bristles. The product, which brings together two of the most commonly used personal hygiene products, is available in vending machines at train stations, airports, bus depots, and in drugstores. The toothbrush has a shelf life of 18 plus months because of its polypropylene packaging.[3]

Consumers are seeking technological advances in self-care and evaluation products. Driven by a shift toward wellness, Americans increasingly desire to discover health problems early. Also, in the face of rising medical costs, consumers see do-it-yourself home diagnostics as a more economical way to answer certain health-related questions.

Hospitals, hoping to cash in on this fast-growing market, have begun to sponsor health fairs and offer free screenings for cholesterol, osteoporosis, and diabetes as well as for prostate, skin, and colorectal cancer. At these events, attendees are shown how they can later test themselves using one of the many home diagnostics the hospital sells.[4] By packaging the knowledge and the test device together, many local providers have successfully created a highly valued package.

DirekTek, one of Europe's largest and most successful computer hardware distributors, always seeks to package the products it offers in a myriad of ways. Most recent packages have included Jade and Saphir desktop scanners from Linotype-Hell with television sets and digital cameras from companies that include Kodak, Polaroid, and Hitachi.

In recent years, several local drive-through lumberyards have opened across the county. For decades, housing contractors chronically complained of the incredible amount of time that they wasted buying building materials. The process can take upwards of half a day as the contractor travels between various supply stores, first buying and then waiting for the materials to be delivered. In bad weather, it can take even more time. The "drive-through" concept greatly enhances convenience, efficiency, and productivity for customers and has led to a dramatic rise in the profitability of such facilities. They provide customers with a one-stop shopping experience that allows them to select, load, and purchase their needed supplies without ever leaving their vehicle.

Russ and Leroy Riva of Canaan, Connecticut, have recently constructed a 50,000-square-foot drive-through lumberyard. Explains Russ about the new facility, "The contractor is in a hurry. It will be awfully nice on a wet, cold day for him to easily pick up all the materials he needs and keep dry. I can't tell you the number of times a customer in the past screamed at us when we couldn't meet their expectations. We have to give the people what they want. We have to integrate everything we offer to the customer."[5]

Each of these examples provides us with a sense of the power an effective package can mean to a product or service.

THE "MAGIC OF 3"

Although the creation of strong packages is a critical first step towards vertical integration, the correct number and typology of packages need to be addressed. Fundamental to successful vertical integration is the ability to offer your product or service at different price points, each of which reflects separate levels of value.

The ability to properly benchmark at different levels needs to be vertical, not horizontal, in nature. Vertical means the packages offered are differentiated by value, not just price. The value added takes priority over all other aspects of the package. Price is only a support in the differentiation of value—nothing else. Those companies that are most successful in getting maximum value for their product or service lead with value, followed only later by price. These leaders are value driven or price driven.

The benefit of a hierarchy of choices makes it much easier to raise prices by adding value or benchmarking rather than simply raising them. Further, study after study shows if products or services are appropriately integrated, customers will generally upgrade themselves to the higher-priced level.

It is important to note that the magic in the Magic of 3 comes from the fact that nearly all consumers are able to clearly envision three choices of a particular product or service. Market research reveals this to be the case in nearly every purchase scenario. Three is a particularly strong quantity because more than three options tend to confuse, while less than three doesn't take full advantage of the consumer's desire for choice, therefore lessening the value proposition.

One of the more widely known illustrations of the Magic of 3 is the way McDonald's initiated the sale of beverages at fast-food restaurants over 30 years ago. Today, small, medium, and large have become so commonplace that this vertical integration strategy is used for literally thousands of products.

For several years, I traveled all over the country working with regional Toro dealer groups to teach them how to sell their products vertically. The focus was not on simply selling a lawn tractor but integrating—packaging—the accessories as part of the sale. Customers were offered the same tractor with three different option packages designed to meet all of their outdoor needs, not simply lawn equipment with an X or Y accessory.

UPS also provides us with a wonderful example of the Magic of 3—next-day, second-day, and ground service. Each service offers a clear, definable choice that is value driven rather than price driven, depending on the needs of the customer.

Boeing's 737 family of planes is the best-selling commercial airliner in history. More people have flown on a Boeing 737 than on any other plane. The current generation is the 300, 400, and 500 series, each of which offers distinct packages dependent on the needs of the buyer.

Hewlett Packard's HP OfficeJet series 500 is a wonderful example of integrating all of the products at your disposal in an all-in-one unit. The 500 series contains HP's first color inkjet printer with fax, copier, and scanning capability. It is a tremendous improvement over the popular 300 series.

Honda has taken its popular Accord line and offered three different packages: the base unit; the LX; and the Accord.

An often-made mistake is overpackaging. Photographers in particular are frequently guilty of this; they fail to recognize the difference between a true package and simply an accessory. Conversely, many consultants lose potential business because they fail to offer more than one or two services.

VALUATING THE CHOICES

The final step for vertical integration is the valuation of the three value-driven packages that are being offered. The strategy uses the following three tactics to achieve this goal:

Step 1: The three packages are divided into A, B, and C.

Step 2: They are organized into a hierarchy where A is of the least value, B is of more value than A but less than C, and C is of the highest value.

Step 3: The pricing spread between A and B is greater than the difference between B and C.

In this methodology, the idea is to create more value on the higher end by offsetting the price difference. The goal is to say to the customer, "By purchasing A, you will receive X benefit. However, for more money you can enjoy B, which will provide X and Y benefits. And for just a little more, you can enjoy C, which has all the benefits of A and B plus Z! Research shows customers will lean toward the higher end if they perceive the difference in value to be greater than the difference in price. Further, it is critical to brand the C choice as the end high and make it the benchmark.

Movie theaters valuate their three beverage sizes—small, medium, and large—in the following way: Small is 99 cents; medium is $1.19; and large is $1.25.

The three delivery options offered by UPS are valuated in the following manner: A ground package is about $6.00; a second-day delivery at about $9.50; and next-day delivery at approximately $10.50.

Boeing's 737 series is value driven within three choices: The 500 is the big brother of the 300 and 400 series, ranging from between $33.5 million to $39.5 million. The mother of the three is the 400, which is priced from $38.5 million to $44.5 million. For just a little more, the high end 300 series is available from $41.5 million to $48.5 million.

UDV Liquors

The latest trend in liquors is high-end tequila, which is creating a new tier in that best-selling category. Ultrapremium tequilas are providing additional growth opportunities in an already healthy market and changing the ways customers view the product. One of the leaders in tequila production has been UDV and its popular Jose Cuervo 1800 line. To capture a larger portion of this growing market, UDV has distinguished its 1800 line of products by using a vertically integrated pricing strategy that is dictated by the aging process. The baseline brand is 1800 Reposado, which retails for $18.99. It normally ages for two to three months. Anejo, the middle brand introduced in 1998, is aged in French oak barrels for a minimum of a year. It is packaged in a decanter similar to the Reposado's, but the labeling is higher-end with a gold seal. Anejo retails for $35 to $40 a bottle. At the ultralevel is the Coleccion line, which ages for more than 18 months and comes in a glass bottle etched in the image of a cave. It sells for about $55 a bottle. The strategy used by UDV has made the move from the lower end to the higher end easier for the new tequila consumer. As Steven Goldstein, vice president of brand publicity for UDV, says, "As consumers' overall appreciation for tequila increases, they become more interested in seeking out better tequila-drinking experiences. What we are seeing is a real consumer shift as they seek out a quality product with a distinctive taste profile and unique product credentials. Offering the three different packages has allowed us to better meet the needs of our customers."[6]

Seven Seas

The popularity of natural solutions to illness has given rise to a successful vertical integration strategy for Seven Seas. As a long-time producer of fish products, Seven Seas saw a growing need on the part of their customers for a more direct way to get the benefits of eating seafood. A few years ago, the company introduced cod-liver oil tablets that provide the recommended daily amount of three nutrients derived from eating fish. At the beginning of 1998, the company came out with high-strength cod-liver oil in capsule form to make swallowing easier. In early 1999, the company launched a new, higher-strength cod-liver oil in liquid form. The liquid contains 40 percent more of the omega 3 nutrients in the tablets and capsules and is much easier to digest. Priced only 15 percent more than the capsules, the initial demand for the liquid has been phenomenal.[7]

Although it may seem silly to state, there are many examples of companies that have failed to analyze the profit margins of each package that is being offered. Before creating a pricing structure around the three packages, please know in advance what the margins for each level are.

SUMMARY

With more companies than ever before competing for the customer's business, it is critical to create an environment in which consumers feel they have all of the control at their disposal. The leaders in their industries are the ones who best provide the marketplace with clear, distinct, and complete choices. Leaders effectively design, manage, coordinate, and complete the entire package that is eventually sold. The imperative of vertical integration accomplishes this critical task. The three elements in vertical integration are:

- Creating packages
- The Magic of 3
- Valuating the choices

CHAPTER 5

Segmenting Your Services to Targeted Customers

"All customers are not equal."
—Thom Winninger

Not every customer wants to be treated the same way. Further, not every customer desires the highest quality and service available nor is every customer looking to shop in a Nordstrom-type environment. Some of your clients may want cash-and-carry, while others hope for service with a smile. Others might be seeking a relationship with you and your products, while another group may just want the product or service itself at that particular moment. To maximize your value, it is necessary to customize the point of transaction based on customer demand.

The point of transaction refers to how the customer wants to purchase your product or service. The shopping environment; the transaction system; the knowledge and support received; and the service-after-sale support are all factors that are looked at quite differently by individual buyers. In buying a new car, some consumers will purchase the vehicle via e-commerce—sight unseen. Others will want to test-drive a variety of vehicles; kick the tires; meet the service manager; and then "cut the deal."

RECOGNIZING THE DIFFERENT CUSTOMER SEGMENTS THAT EXIST FOR YOUR PRODUCT OR SERVICE

The incredible variety of customers in the United States makes it incumbent on businesses to segment their product and response to different categories of customer demands. Product and service segmentation is all around us. The SUV market, once dominated by midsize vehicles like the Chevy Blazer and the Ford Explorer, now consists of multiple entries—cheap small, expensive small, cheap midsize, standard midsize, premium midsize, big, and premium big.

Segmentation is quite complex. To add to its difficulty is the fact that the United States will become a nonmajority country in which no single ethnic group will compose more than 50 percent of the population in the next 15 years. The fastest-growing segments are Asian and Pacific Islanders. The U.S. government forecasts the Hispanic population will exceed the Afro-American population by 2013 with 42.1 million persons. Also, family structure has dramatically changed in recent years. Since 1970, the number of married-couple families has risen by more than 20 percent and the number of female-headed families by 122 percent.

Supermarket wholesalers and retailers attending the General Merchandise Marketing Conference in Orlando in early 2000 were urged to recognize the growing multicultural marketplace or else risk misdirected marketing campaigns.

Obviously, all customers are *not* equal. In a marketing campaign geared for a geographic region, for instance, a Hispanic market segment might respond in a particular manner because of its culture and the experience of the group. The Asian and Pacific Islander segment might respond to the same campaign in very different ways, based on their collective backgrounds. Single mothers, given their special roles, might react to the campaign or promotion in a different fashion than other heads of households. And so on . . .

Most companies acknowledge the importance of the distinguishing attributes of individual customers but fail to build their products or services around them. However, based on my work with thousands of companies all over North America, I am convinced most companies are still coming up short in properly targeting their products or services to different categories of customer demands.

If, for example, Wal-Mart or Home Depot or Old Navy would carpet their stores with plush peach, their businesses could suffer. Sam Walton recognized this and realized such surroundings would send the wrong signal to the price-conscious shopper. Further, if Nordstrom or The Gap or Ace Hardware would have concrete-only floors, each would also be sending the wrong message. At its core, segmentation is a matching game where you identify customer demand categories and then segment product and response models to best serve each category.

Critical to this process is the realization that all customers within a particular market segment are not the same. Many companies are quite strong in determining the particular segments of customers but very weak in understanding the differences *within* the segments themselves.

Inside the Hispanic market segment of grocery shoppers, for example, there are several different types of customer—each type with different needs and expectations. Not all Asian Americans will like, want, or demand the same products in the same store. Single mothers will look at a given product or service in a myriad of ways. Simply stated, not all customers within a given market segment are equal. Unfortunately, most companies fail to realize this and end up squandering critical resources.

Too many companies waste time and money on large numbers of customers who couldn't care less about the additional benefits they get. In many cases, customers like these are not profit centers and may even be losers for a company's bottom line. Disheartingly, for a huge percentage of American firms, billions of dollars and millions of human hours are tossed to the wind as they blindly attempt to treat all of their customers as their best clients. Many companies have given all of their customers the same phone number to call for customer service, mistakenly treating their least profitable customers the same as their most profitable ones.

After years of this futility, some companies are finally starting to realize the error of their ways. Across the country, businesses that once sought to capture any customer at any price are concluding the any-customer-is-a-good-one strategy may not have been the right idea.

Dorothy Lane Markets

Norman Mayne, CEO of Dorothy Lane Markets, a grocer in Dayton, Ohio, decided a decade ago to weed out all customers who didn't care about anything but lower prices. "Whenever we ran ads offering a special on pork-and-beans, all we did was attract 'cherry-pickers,'" Mayne says. "It was an exercise in futility. It was a headache for us—and for our regular customers."[1]

AT&T and Sprint

AT&T and Sprint are beginning to cater to their big-spending premium category by having an actual operator answer their calls, while everybody else has to talk to the computer. Meanwhile, some observers worry that MCI, long the best hope of average phone users, will drop residential service altogether in favor of more lucrative business customers.

Citibank

Citibank, the nation's second largest bank, has increased the minimum balance for a no-fee checking account to $7,500. Citibank management is trying to identify the customer category that wants to do more business with the bank. Credit card debt, mortgage loans, deposits, and investments can be counted toward the minimum. The initiative pushes away the costly small-account customers who don't want to, or can't, meet the minimum service amounts. An unintended benefit may very well be the departure of customers who take away from, rather than add to, the bottom line.

MGM Grand

The Las Vegas casinos are demonstrating a trend toward the segmentation of guests after years of trying to cater to all visitors by using the same methods. MGM Grand, Inc., has been focusing its energies on a precious piece of its business: the high-roller crowd. As Las Vegas's building boom continues, MGM has decided to invest $150 million to build a 29-villa deluxe hotel next to its 5,005-rooom flagship on The Strip. The villas are free—but only for those with credit lines of at least $1 million. Villa guests will be picked up at the airport in Mercedes limos and whisked by butlers to their laps of luxury. Villa sizes range from 2,500 to 12,000 square feet; 11 of the villas have indoor pools.[2]

Smart companies are the ones that don't throw away their best response, service, or product on customers who will never appreciate it. Instead, leaders focus their greatest energy on their premium customers and streamline basic resources to nonpremium customers. Leaders understand what sets their premium customers apart from the rest of their clientele. They then construct different levels of service and product integrity around these variances.

Differentiating customer categories within market segments is a fundamental necessity for today's ultracompetitive market conditions. In many cases, the capacity for a firm to properly target its customers within a particular segment and provide them with different levels of benchmarked benefits will often mark the line between long-term success and failure.

The tactics used for appropriately targeting your product or service to different categories or levels of demand within a given segment are threefold: first, the recognition of the different customer segments that exist for your product or service; second, the determination of the various levels or categories within each market segment; and third, the creation of benchmark responses to the differentiated groups within the segment.

THE DETERMINATION OF CATEGORIES WITHIN CUSTOMER SEGMENTS

As mentioned previously, market segments are all around us. As a demographic group, the 280 million residents of the United States provide companies with an innumerable amount of market segments for their products or services. The sheer size and diversity of the nation make it a formidable task for companies to determine which are the precise market segments for what they have to sell.

Eight hundred and thirty-two consumer magazines were launched in 1999, backed by a $12.7 billion magazine advertising market; and Samir Husni, University of Mississippi professor of journalism, estimates 1,000 new launches by the end of 2000. A trend exists in both consumer and business-to-business magazines toward segmenting the magazine market into very specific groups.

Geographically and demographically, the United States is a vast and widely varied country. For instance, the differences in weather between Minnesota and Alabama are immense. To describe the weather as hot means something completely different to someone living in Minneapolis versus a resident of Birmingham. Hot might be 85° in my hometown, whereas it could be described as cool or refreshing in Alabama in the summertime. A snowstorm in Minneapolis is assuredly different from a snowstorm in Birmingham. Anyone who does business across America can most certainly tell you the differences between their customers or suppliers in New York, Omaha, and Los Angeles.

Many businesses erroneously try to plow forward into the marketplace like a farmer who always fails in growing corn on his land instead of analyzing which other crop might grow there. They focus on having great products rather than great customers. From my point of view, I'd always prefer to have great customers. Great customers who come to you looking for products and services will always be more profitable than great products on your shelf waiting to be purchased. Focusing on great customers instead of great products is the difference between working with buying power or working with cost.

An aging population has led to the creation of a wide array of market segments of adults, creating new and dynamic segments of customers that never existed before. Moreover, within these segments are different levels of customer satisfaction that I consider and call *categories*.

Happy Trails Golf Shop

The senior segment of golfers, for instance, defined as age 50 and older, has grown by 16 percent in the past decade to 6.4 million golfers and 26 percent of the market. It is the only segment to have grown within the golfing public. In addition, the older set spends more than 50 percent more money on golf than all the other segments together. John Bishop, head professional at Happy Trails Golf Club in Sun City, Arizona, has been successfully selling to the 50 plus crowd for more than 17 years. He attributes his success to the realization that older golfers are quite different and have different needs than younger ones. As an example, retired men have a lifetime's worth of golf shirts in the closet. Bishop recently ran a charity event where each old golf shirt donated to charity was worth $5 off a new shirt. Seniors aren't cheap, Bishop explains, but they're value conscious. Ninety percent of Bishop's wood sales are from custom-fitted clubs, which run upwards of $1,000. With focus on presale and follow-up service, Bishop creates the value needed for this lucrative segment.[3]

Mueller Sports Medicine

The aging population's desire to stay fit is fueling growth in the support, brace, and tape segments of the sports medicine industry.

The result of the rise in activity is also a growing rise in injuries. It is estimated there are more than 25,000 ankle injuries every day in the United States—a larger percentage occurring in the over-50 segment than in any other. Mueller Sports Medicine has seen its sales expand 15 percent annually as it has introduced a number of new items. Most successful has been a hinged knee device that is intended to operate as three braces in one for older customers.[4]

Teenagers spend tens of billions of their own dollars as well as greater chunks of their family's income every day. Younger children are also becoming an increasingly important segment as they directly influence billions of dollars of their parents' disposable income.

Studio photographers have identified a number of market segments that are portrait sensitive. However, photographers must be aware that there are those who want a total program, those who only want a choice program with multiple packages, and those who merely want to point and click their own digital camera so they can download the image and print it out on their color printer. A full-service studio will go out of business if it attempts to serve all of these categories with the same level of response and product.

Rural, suburban, and urban residents are each segments distinguished to some extent by the place where they live. Custom builders account for 34.5 percent of the National Association of Home Builders members, its largest segment. Within this custom group, different demands come from customers primarily dependent upon whether they live in the country, the suburbs, or cities. Customers are often finicky and demanding, but they promise big profits for builders who understand their specific needs and wants.[5] The right kind of demanding customer can mean higher prices and bigger margins.

Businesses, too, are an assorted group. Small, medium, and large companies look at their respective roles in the marketplace from very different perspectives. Home-based firms are the fastest growing business segment—in fact, they are creating a new segment altogether. Still, the jury remains out on the long-term profitability of this segment whose status appears to trend toward the transaction, low profit, level.

United Airlines

United Airlines has spent about $30 million over the past year on its Economy Plus program in order to give its best customers up to six inches more leg room in coach class. United chose to reconfigure the first 6 to 11 rows in its economy class sections instead of expanding its first-class section. Its approach differs from other airlines that say they'll keep their best customers loyal by giving them more chances to get a first-class seat.

Economy Plus "is to reward and retain our most loyal customers, the business flier," says United President Rono Dutta. Fliers who pay for the higher classes of business fares represent about 6 percent of United's passengers but more than 37 percent of its revenues. The Economy Plus seats will have a seat pitch of 35 or 36 inches, the distance from the back of the seat to the front of the seat ahead of it. Pitch in most coach sections is less than 30 inches.

The seats were designed for the benefit of its Premiere Mileage Plus members—fliers who put in at least 25,000 paid miles a year on United or its Star Alliance partners—Air Canada, Air New Zealand, Ansett, Luftansa, SAS, Thai, and Varig. Passengers who buy full-fare economy tickets can also request Economy Plus.

Dutta says United's move was intended to address the dilemma many frequent fliers face when trying to get an increasingly difficult upgrade. "So many of our most frequent fliers say they can't get an upgrade into first class. Economy Plus is meant to give them that option."

In an effort to not alienate their first-class and business-class passengers, United's first-class and business-class sections will still be used for the elite traveler. Moreover, elite-level members will be able to reserve Economy Plus seats no matter how much they paid for their ticket. And United frequent fliers can use their miles to get an Economy Plus seat if space is available. Also, if a United flight takes off with some Economy Plus seats, United will let coach-class passengers move up to them.[6]

Whatever the product or service being offered, it is critical for a company to identify the current and potential customer segments that exist for it. It is not enough, however, to simply identify which are the market segments for your product or service. To maximize your value and achieve full price, it is incumbent to profile the types of customers that are contained within a particular market segment.

Market segmentation alone can be dangerous. It accomplishes the task of placing all of your customers into nice, organized groups. However, it also puts marginal customers on the same pedestal that should be reserved exclusively for your premium customers. Remember, it is understanding and fulfilling the highest needs of your *premium customers* that will get you closer to full price for your product or service than any other single activity. Anything that gets in the way between you and your premium customers must be dealt with. Customer segmentation, if not handled properly, can falsely lead companies down a primrose path from which recovery is long and expensive.

Based on my work with some of America's most successful firms, the best practice for analyzing your customers within market segments and locating your premium customers is to place them into one of three categories: *relationship, choice,* or *transaction.* Once this is accomplished, it will be much easier to benchmark your service and product levels differently to each group within the particular segment—always keeping your premium customers closest to you.

The deciding factor of where to place your customers should be the amount of demand and potential loyalty they have for your product or service. In other words, what is the potential of developing a relationship after the sale? For purposes of description, relationship customers have the highest level of intensity for what you have to offer. They want service, information, and support after the sale. They are the premium customers, as discussed earlier.

The second category—choice customers—purchase the product and everything else that goes with it but nothing else. They don't necessarily need support after the sale. They will seek choice, price, and availability from you and your competitors. They like the flexibility that comes with choice. If they do buy, they are strong solid customers. However, their intensity and loyalty after the sale is not nearly as strong as those of relationship customers.

The final category—transaction customers—have the least amount of attachment to your product or service. They make up the segment that is solely driven by price or some other minimal factor that does nothing to add to your future relationship. They want the product and nothing more.

Relationship customers buying a computer would be interested in the total system to satisfy all of their needs, including design applications and software. Choice category customers would want a selection of computers at different price points and speeds. They compare the price against the package. They will be concerned about the setup after the sale. And transaction category customers would surf the Net looking for the best price for the hard drive, zip drive, monitor, and modem. They want a deal from whoever can supply it as long as it's shipped "overnight.com."

The "Play-It-Again" market segment is quite familiar to those families with kids who are playing sports. Relationship customers want "Play-It-Again" to be their supplier of both new and used sporting goods as the kids grow up. Relationship customers will trade in their used equipment for new upgrades—creating great value for the store as they turn over the smaller for the bigger.

Relationship customers want all the help and information they can get. To retain this category, "Play-It-Again" maintains size data on each kid and lists of Little League equipment requirements as well as offering a fix-it service and help with sizing and fitting.

It never ceases to amaze me how many companies determine their monthly profit and loss by looking at the total revenue from all of their customer categories. Relationship and choice customers should deliver the highest profit margins—with the emphasis, of course, on the relationship profile. If your company is being supported primarily by transaction customers, it is crucial to shift away from them toward your more loyal clients to ensure stability and long-term success.

Transaction customers are flippant and change with the wind to the lowest priced supplier. Nothing you do will ever build value with this group. It doesn't matter what you try. Transaction customers simply don't care. To construct your business plan around them is utter folly. The only way to make money from this category is to have the lowest price. This is a tactic, not a strategy, and only one player in each sector can maintain the price position.

THE CREATION OF BENCHMARK RESPONSES TO CUSTOMER CATEGORIES

Once you have determined which customers are in which particular category, it is necessary to benchmark your response, product, and service to each profile.

For many firms, benchmarking services and products to transaction customers is a difficult undertaking. Some companies choose not to even address the transaction customer. They disregard the transaction customer and cater only to the relationship and choice customers. Other businesses are now pushing their transaction customers toward catalogs on CD-ROM, telephone ordering, and the Internet—concentrating on e-commerce—to reduce transaction costs as a way to deal with this category.

For those firms that decide to serve the transaction customer, Warehouse Up Box Stores provide a good case study on how to control them. When you walk into one of its facilities, you are immediately struck by the no-frills environment. The merchandise is offered in large quantities with a limited selection. There is very little staff support; you must pack the merchandise yourself after going through the line at the centralized checkout.

Airlines have been successfully categorizing their customers through frequent-flyer programs. Although every passenger on a given flight embarks on the same plane from the same city and arrives at the same destination, each passenger looks at the level of service quite differently. Of course, first-class, business-class, and economy are three discernible customer categories within the plane. However, a better gauge for the airline in profiling customers has been through the creation of frequent-flyer categories.

Northwest Airlines

As a Minneapolis resident, I do the vast majority of my flying with Northwest. Like all the major airlines, Northwest categorizes its customers primarily based on the number of miles a customer has traveled with it in a given year. Platinum, gold, and silver categories have been created by Northwest as ways to differentiate their frequent-flying customers. Platinum-level flyers are able to request free upgrades 72 hours in advance of a flight, whereas gold-level customers get 24 hours prior to departure and silver the same day to ask for an upgrade. Further, platinum customers get a different phone number to call to ensure a faster response. This example is what I label as three levels of a benchmarked response to customer categories.

Marriott International

The success of Marriott as America's leading hotel chain is due largely to its ability to identify its customer categories within the all-important business traveler segment. Marriott has developed three profile levels of business travelers and benchmarked them through the creation of not only frequent traveler categories but also product categories such as their Residence Inns, Courtyards, and Fairfield Inns. In most major cities, all three can be found within a four-mile radius of each other, but they are not in direct competition with each other, as it may seem.

A Residence Inn creates an apartment atmosphere with fireplaces, living rooms, and kitchens. It is designed for both upscale travelers and those who are staying in town for an extended period of time. A Courtyard is a full-service hotel with a restaurant, large exercise room, and spacious guest suites. A Fairfield Inn typically has a small pool, no restaurant service, and standard rooms. Although all are Marriott properties, each hotel category offers a customized option to a particular type of business traveler depending on the traveler's specific needs. As a result, Marriott is able to capture an even larger percentage of business travelers.

The remainder of the hospitality industry in North America has followed Marriott's lead and begun to focus on targeted customers within the business traveler segment. The top segments by hotels rooms under construction in America are extended-stay, 38,228; luxury/first class, 28,270; and midmarket limited service, 26,141.[7]

Much like traditional lodging, the vacation ownership industry is also segmenting its product within different category benchmarks. Marriott Vacation Club has tapped into a loyal clientele stemming from powerful brand equity and a rich heritage enjoyed by its resorts. To complement its current time-share offerings in the quality tier, Marriott recently recognized a growing demand for a moderately priced time-share and rolled out Horizons By Marriott Vacation Club.[8]

"It's been a long time coming, and it's evolved through customer research," said Ed Kinnney, senior director of brand advertising of Marriott Vacation Club. "We realized it's time to diversify and open up other audiences. It's very similar to what we at Marriott did years ago with traditional lodging, being a pioneer in multiple tiers, which worked well."[9] Marriott's moderate vacation ownership resorts range from about $9,000 to $13,000, while the quality tier can range from $17,500 to $48,000.

Carson Vacation Ownership

Dave Gandrud, director of marketing services for Minneapolis-based Carson Vacation Ownership, said the company has rolled out a time-share version of its successful line of hotels. Carlson will offer multitier products to multidevelopers and franchisers. Three distinct price points targeting all sectors will parallel the company's broad spectrum of resort offerings:

1. The Club Regent—an exclusive ultraluxury, high-end offering targeting individuals with a high net worth. A membership offers two-week to four-week intervals in excess of $100,000.

2. A yet-to-be-named high-end luxury brand ranging from $18,000 to $75,000
3. Radisson Vacation Villas upscale first-class units from $10,000 to $20,000

Gandrud adds that this multitier approach allows the company to leverage what its hotel brands have already defined.[10]

As the benchmarked response moves closer to the relationship customer, the attention becomes more personal. Distributors, for example, in the relationship category benchmark their response by providing order-entry software to customers, actually managing the inventory supply after it arrives to a customer's location.

Patterson Dental

Patterson Dental, one of the nation's leading suppliers to dentists, calls its relationship category Patterson Plus. It offers total supply sourcing, a territory specialist, and a supply system, all to ensure that dentists never run out of the materials they need.

Taco Bell

After finding out the needs of its most important customers—customers between 18 and 24 years old—Taco Bell has concluded it wants more from its fast-food experience than it's gotten so far. The upshot: Young adults today have hedonistic impulses and seek maximum stimulation from rich-tasting food, even when they have only a couple of bucks to spend. "We're tapping into this new trend by introducing a self-indulgent, heavy-in-taste called the Chulupa," says Mary Wagner, chief technology and quality officer at Taco Bell. "The heavy users of Taco Bell crave more flavor, extremely rich, spicy, and indulgent products." Taco Bell is offering three versions of the new item: Supreme, Baja, and Santa Fe. Each is priced at 99 cents.[11]

SUMMARY

Not every customer wants to be treated the same way. Further, not every customer desires the highest quality and service available. Differentiating targeted customer categories within market segments is a fundamental necessity for today's ultracompetitive market conditions. The tactics surrounding the appropriate targeting of your product or service to different categories or levels of demand within a given segment are these:

- The recognition of different customer segments that exist for your product or service

- The determination of various levels or categories within each market segment

- The creation of benchmark responses to differentiated groups within each segment

CHAPTER 6

Owning the Customer's Buying Cycle

"Even before we sell a customer something, we instinctively know we have to get the customer back again and again and again."

—Thom Winninger

For any company that is trying to acquire new customers, which is pretty much every company, we know the costs associated with the identification, communication, and capturing of these new clients is very high. In fact, some companies are known to spend upwards of 35 percent of every revenue dollar on acquiring first-time customers. In far too many cases, the costs of acquisition are so high that if large numbers of first-time customers don't return, the company might quite possibly go out of business. The most valuable customers—those who keep you in business and guarantee future profits—are those who buy from you again and again and again.

The cosmetic industry understands this reality very well. Cosmetics are almost the perfect product. They are used up quickly, improve the way you feel about yourself, and are easily connected to other products that can be packaged together or added on. Further, cosmetics also enjoy some degree of brand loyalty.

Nevertheless, even in the cosmetics industry, it is still not good enough to do the best job once, twice, or even three times. Customer loyalty today depends, to a great extent, on anticipating the customer's needs and buying cycles as the way to reduce transaction costs and own—that is, control—the customer's buying cycle.

It is certainly a buyer's market out there. Britt Wood, director of research technology for the International Mass Retail Association may sum it up best when he states, "We have entered the century of the consumers—and consumers know it. They know that collectively they can make or break a company, and they expect retailers and vendors to meet their expectations. Those firms that do the best job of catering to their wishes will be rewarded with their dollars." [1]

Smart companies in the new millennium are those that do the following when it comes to building customer loyalty:

- Smart companies anticipate when and how a customer buys.
- Smart companies identify shopping frequency.
- Smart companies build an accumulating incentive program that rewards the customer for frequent and multiple purchases rather than for a single transaction.
- Smart companies offer an ordering system tailored to the specific needs of the customer.
- Smart companies, where possible, create a consumable product with a "use-it-up" philosophy.

Computer lease programs over a 24-month period that offer technology upgrades at various intervals are ways smart companies build loyalty. A distributor inventory management program that insures an uninterrupted stream of supply is another. Whatever the business model, constructing strategy around the proactive acquisition of the customer's loyalty is a necessity. Unfortunately, such a perspective is less common than it should be.

For the past ten Novembers, I have bought two cords of wood for my fireplace from the same guy. It never ceases to astound me that every year I have to make a concerted effort to call the "wood guy" the third week of November to receive my annual supply. If I didn't call *him* each year to purchase *his* product, no relationship would exist between us at all.

Every autumn for the past decade, I have waited with anticipation for the wood guy to do something that recognizes my value to him as a customer. Unfortunately, this annual event always results in the same scenario: no response from him whatsoever until I make the call. He seems like a nice guy and seems genuinely interested in how my family enjoys our fireplace. Nevertheless, after he unloads the truck and I give him the check, he shakes my hand, wishes me Happy Holidays, and drives away. My heart always sinks a little as I instinctively know I would never see the wood guy again unless I initiate the contact.

In my travels and work with companies all across North America, it never ceases to amaze me how many multi-million-dollar firms do business in the same way as the wood guy. These companies depend on their customers to come back and buy again rather than trying to own each customer's buying cycle. Barbara Kaplan, a partner with Yankelovich Partners, the global research firm, says, "Consumers are very feisty, very self-reliant, and very smart. And out of this self-reliance comes a sense of control." "There's a new sense of power in the consumer's gut," Kaplan adds. "The message to business is this: 'You meet my needs or you're toast!' "

On top of these demands from consumers, research is showing that as the population ages, Americans are spending less of their leisure time shopping. A direct result is that retailers and vendors are seeing fewer frequent shoppers. For most companies, the drop-off in frequent shoppers is especially noticeable. According to one of the most comprehensive surveys in recent years of consumers' shopping habits, the firm of PricewaterhouseCooper interviewed 6,200 Americans and discovered that the vast majority of consumers tend to purchase at the first store they visit, with from one-half to two-thirds making a purchase at the first store they enter. The research suggests nearly 75 percent of hardware and tool buyers make purchases at the first store they enter, while more than 50 percent of consumer electronics buyers stop at two or more stores before they purchase an item. And two-thirds of the shoppers surveyed visited only one store when purchasing beds and bath linens.

As I have already discussed, there are strategies that firms of all sizes can implement to meet the demands of this new breed of customer. In addition to leading the field, selling the program, vertical integration, and segmenting to targeted customers, enlightened companies and individuals also recognize the critical importance of owning the customer's buying cycle.

Owning the customer's buying cycle is fundamental to attracting and maintaining the best customers of your product or service.

Three ways in which the smartest companies and individuals own the customer's buying cycle, or loop, are (1) offering accumulative incentives with every purchase; (2) effectively managing the after-purchase needs of the customer; and (3) proactively anticipating future purchases.

OFFERING ACCUMULATIVE INCENTIVES

A "build-type" incentive does exactly that. It builds on the already existing relationship in ways that increase the amount of affiliation and loyalty the customer has with your product or service. Such build-type incentives are meant to keep customers in the loop. Frequent-flyer miles and punchcards for coffee purchases or car washes are all common ways in which companies seek to build incentives into the relationships with their customers.

The number of U.S. supermarkets offering card-based customer loyalty programs has risen six percentage points from 54 to 60 percent in just the past year, according to the Cox Direct Survey of Promotional Practices. The survey also revealed that 78 percent of shoppers belong to more than one frequent-shopper program.

CBS SportsLine.com

CBS SportsLine has established a customer loyalty program to enhance its e-commerce initiative and build membership. Sports-

Line Rewards is a free program that gives members points every time they view a page on CBS SportsLine.com, the Web site devoted to sports information, entertainment, and merchandise. Members earn one point for each page they view.

SportsLine.com currently has 60,000 members. Visitors can view certain information for free but are charged $4.95 a month for more customized information. The points can be used to receive "hot pick" rewards, such as online chats with Michael Jordan, e-mails from Shaquile O'Neal, and backstage passes to concerts. Team jerseys, memorabilia, and food are among the 750 gifts available. Rewards change daily, so members are encouraged to visit the site each day.

Neiman Marcus

When Sara M. Dunham regularly drives the seven hours from her home in Baton Rouge to spend about $200,000 a year at the Neiman Marcus store in Dallas, the rewards for her purchases go far beyond the jewelry and furs she buys. As a member of the In Circle, the Neiman Marcus frequent-shopper club, she and her husband will be treated to a free week in Milan with first-class flights and hotels. Last year it was Paris.

Green Hills Farms

Green Hills Farm in Syracuse, New York, the northeastern supermarket chain, consistently has one of the top frequent-shopper programs in the world, particularly because of its short-term promotions that have dramatic impacts on the store's high-spending customers. Gary Hawkins, operator of the chain, says, "Using a loyalty card as a program for continuity makes the difference."[2]

Hawkins recently compiled the figures from a recent promotion, which reveal that the top tier of loyalty cardholders increased their spending by more than 20 percent over the ten-week offer period.

The promotion offered a reduced-price Italian cookware set worth about $83, with the level of discount pricing dependent on the cardholder's total spending over the ten weeks of the offer. (See the following table.) Customers spending at least $1,000 over the promotion time received the cookware for free.

10 Weeks' Spending	Reward Discount	Additional Return on Spending
Up to $399	0%	0.0%
$400–$599	25	5.2
$600–$799	50	6.9
$800–$999	75	7.9
Over $1,000	100	8.3

Source: Data Works Marketing Group.

The program was completed in ten weeks, and although only 18 percent of Green Hill's recognized households participated in the promotion, in those ten weeks they accounted for 61 percent of total sales. In addition to higher revenues, Hawkins pointed out that targeting high-spending customers with the promotion also impacted gross profits, as these customers tended to purchase more high-margin products.

The return on investment for the promotion—notwithstanding any intangible benefits such as increased customer satisfaction or higher average loyalty after the promotion ended—was 105 percent![3]

Musicland Stores

U.S. home entertainment retailer Musicland Stores Corporation has extended its Replay customer loyalty program to its On Cue chain of stores. The program, which currently operates only in the Sam Goody outlets of the corporation, has more than half a million members and will now be available in more than 850 stores across the country. Customers who take part in the loyalty program receive benefits that include a personalized Replay newsletter carrying entertainment news and information, and members-only Replay Weekends when members can earn extra bonus points and discounts on purchases.[4]

National Association of Chain Drug Stores

The National Association of Chain Drug Stores (NACDS) has developed and implemented a card-based, customer loyalty program for its members. The goal is to help chains increase nonpharmacy sales and reinforce the loyalty of its customers by working with Consumer Card Marketing Inc. (CCMI) and seeking manufacturers to participate in the program.

AutoNation Inc.

AutoNation, the world's largest automotive retailer, has launched its new customer loyalty program called "AutoRewards." The program's aims are to redefine the car purchase experience and make every AutoNation customer a customer for life. The program will use a blend of customer recognition and extra value rewards to encourage customers to increase their usage of AutoNation USA's products and services, which along with new and used car sales include maintenance, vehicle rentals, and accessories.

Ames Department Stores

Each spring, in anticipation of the upcoming baseball season, Ames Department Stores, Inc., of Rocky Hill, Connecticut, invites Little League coaches to conduct their team sign-ups at local outlets. Little Leaguers are issued a 25 percent savings card on all baseball-related products, with 30 percent saving for purchases over $100.

American Express

Credit card firms, experiencing decreasing margins, have been making efforts at offering services that build value, including new customer loyalty programs. American Express (AMEX) recently added 14 new partners to its Membership Rewards program. Avis Rent-a-Car and Cathay Pacific Airlines are new partners in the travel sector. AMEX is already allied with 13 airlines and the Latin Pass frequent-flyer program; 5 major hotel chains; the top 4 car rental agencies; 200 resorts; and retail firms outside of the travel sector.

Diners Club

Meanwhile, the Diners Club Tailored Travel customer loyalty program is the most extensive among credit card vendors with redemption through 24 air carriers and 11 large hotel chains. Walter Sanders, vice president for corporate affairs for Diners Club says of their successful program, "We give our best customers the double luxury of convenience and time saved."[5]

With such programs, it is important to realize it's not the quality of the items or their diversity but rather the quality of their appeal. Starbucks, for example, offers a simple punch card that builds to a free cup of coffee after ten purchases.

American Cyanamid

A recent ad campaign for American Cyanamid Company's Harvest Partners customer loyalty program shows a farmer surveying a crop of shiny tools sprouting from a soybean field. The advertisement is designed to keep farmers buying Cyanamid's crop protection products. Loyal customers can qualify to receive premiums such as tools, savings bonds, and college scholarships as well as hunting and fishing adventure trips.

Although each one of these illustrations provides us with tremendous insight into how smart companies maintain the all-important frequency of purchase, a critical factor in their success needs to be recognized. Mark Twain is quoted as saying, "When you find yourself in the majority, pause and reflect." The widespread proliferation of incentive-based customer loyalty programs compels us to ask: If almost everyone is going to these programs, where is the extra value for the customer? And aren't these programs becoming commodities rather than attempts to capture the customer's buying cycle?

It is not critical that the program is based on a card, but the program must have a way in which customers can track the accumulation of their incentives. Human nature dictates that in most cases purchases will increase when customers understand how close they are to receiving an award. Blockbuster's 'Free Video' program is generally ineffective because it is based on a surprise. Customers have no idea when their next free video is coming. Therefore, why would a customer rent that one extra video to win the next free one?

The ability to provide your customers exactly what they are really looking for is essential in building a viable, long-term incentive-based program. The best way to achieve this is by offering a "pure item" as an incentive that meets a regular want or need. Pure items are directly related to a customer's primary purchase—a coffee grinder for coffee; lubricants for lawn mowers; or a meal for a restaurant customer.

Airline frequent-flyer miles are probably the best example of a pure item. For many customers, airline travel—whether for business or pleasure—is constant and ongoing. Free gasoline or rebates toward car purchases can also be described as pure items. They bring the purchase closer to the intimate wants or needs of your customer. The use of pure items more often than not characterizes the most successful customer loyalty programs in the marketplace.

EFFECTIVELY MANAGING THE CUSTOMER'S AFTER-PURCHASE NEEDS

The back end of a sale, sometimes referred to as the "be-backs," enhances the long-term relationships with your customers and is critical in owning the buying cycle. If you buy a lawn mower, what about the engine lubricants that are needed for the regular maintenance of the unit? Who will sell them? What about the annual servicing that is recommended for the blades? And what about additional accessories like a snowplow or garden tiller? Which company will capture this additional business and better own the buying cycle? To be a leader, it is necessary to match after-purchase products or services with the needs of your customers. Remember, the more you are involved in their buying process, the more likely you are to achieve full price. Servicing the furnace after installation, providing salt for the water softener, and selling toner cartridges for the copier bring you closer to the customer's buying cycle.

Texas Drug Warehouse

Texas Drug Warehouse has started carrying sports supplements and nutritional products in its stores to attract sports-minded customers and increase sales among ordinary shoppers. The stores have set aside 12- to 16-foot spaces to showcase the products. It has worked to offer pricing competitive with General Nutrition Centers, according to Mark Metzger, senior buyer of the chain. Besides its high profit potential, sports nutrition also has the ability to generate increased store traffic and draw new customers. "There is a very high level of repeat sales in sports nutrition. A 5-pound can of whey protein might last a body builder 10 days, whereas a 90-tablet bottle of Centrum will last three months."[6]

Technology is without question transforming all of our lives in a variety of ways. It has enabled businesses to learn more about their customers and better manage their buying cycles. However, in an ever-increasing number of situations, technology is dampening after-purchase sales.

The auto industry is full of such examples. General Motors recently announced that in forthcoming years, it would install a computerized oil monitoring system on 90 percent of its vehicles. The system works by tracking the number of engine revolutions and such factors as operating temperatures to determine when the engine's oil requires changing. A "change oil" message is then flashed on the dashboard. The system, when completely operational, promises slashing oil usage by 10 million gallons in the year 2003, with the decreases growing every subsequent model year. This technological development will negatively impact motor oil sales and service centers that perform the change. In addition to motor oil, three spark plug vendors—Autolite, Bosch, and Splitfire—have already introduced platinum-tipped spark plugs with long-life warranties. Long life is also evident in antifreeze; Prestone markets its long-life version that is good for 150,000 miles, up from 100,000 in March of 1997.[7]

Despite the changes in technology, Jim Lind Amoco of Waterloo, Iowa, has a program service relationship that reminds us how simple it can be to keep good customers. Jim regularly sends a personalized notice of the service sequence on the automobile. Jim also delivers the newly serviced vehicle to the customer only after it has been run through his car wash.

PROACTIVELY ANTICIPATING FUTURE PURCHASES

It is necessary that businesses keep customers "in the loop" when it comes to anticipating future needs. A Minneapolis winter is difficult to describe to anyone unfamiliar with the northern exposure. Needless to say, one of the most important factors to surviving months of subzero temperatures and blinding snow is a good furnace. Throughout our city, successful furnace stores contact their customers every September to arrange an inspection of their furnaces for the following month. This anticipation of a future purchase based on climatic change brings these leaders closer to their customers.

Penn Cycles

Penn Cycles of Minneapolis is rated one of the top ten bicycle stores in America. Elmer Sorenson, its founder, has devised a program that captures his customer's attention through its emphasis on the after-purchase sale. The Preferred Cyclist Card entitles bike buyers to special pricing on the store's best-selling accessories.

Accessory	Regular Price	Preferred Cyclist Card Price
Helmet	$39.99	$26.99
Water Bottle	3.99	1.99
Water Bottle Cage	7.99	5.39
Cycling Gloves	16.99	11.69
Bike Lube	3.99	3.14
Tool Bag	17.99	8.99
Bike Shorts	39.99	35.99
Floor Pump	39.99	26.99
Sensor Cycling Computer	39.99	22.49
Dual Saddle	24.99	17.99
Rear Carrier	39.99	22.49
Headlight	19.99	14.39
Lock	39.99	31.49

Jubilation

Elaine Powell and Suzanne Levine's Jubilation, a specialty store in Newton, Massachusetts, features unique handmade American crafts and accessories. In 1998 the two women opened a 400-square-foot At Home center next to their already successful 1,000-square-foot outlet. Growth has been fantastic in recent years. According to Powell, the success is directly related to their ability to capture the customer's buying cycle through repeat sales. By offering unique merchandise, the stock is turned every few weeks. Doing so creates a new shopping experience for their customers each time they visit the stores. Such dedication to fashioning a different inventory for their customers gives their customers a reason to come back again and again.

Daewoo Motor

In an innovative plan to boost its number of regular customers, Daewoo Motor America guarantees strong trade-in values of cars sold to students. To anticipate the next purchase, a student who trades in a Daewoo after two or three years for a new one will be guaranteed the same percentage of retained value as the category leader.

Bellcore

George Heilmier, president and chief executive officer of the newly commercialized Bellcore, explains his company's success as a result of its ability to anticipate customer needs and problems and using this in its marketing efforts. Though many companies see customer care as an expense and try to minimize it, Heilmier thinks that Bellcore's approach is necessary in today's highly competitive environment. One of the keys is doing a better job of understanding specific customer needs and acting in a quasi-real-time mode.

Lowe's

For the past several years, Lowe's marketing message about its hardware stores has been shaped by information collected about customers' buying habits based on such factors as cash register transactions and direct mail response cards. These efforts, according to senior management, however, are not enough. "Twenty-five percent of the customers who walk into our stores leave without finding what they came for," says Dale Pond, the company's executive VP of marketing and merchandising.

Now Lowe's wants to move into what Pond labels "Act II" of its marketing effort, from initiation to motivation. "This goes to understanding trends; we need to fall into a creative mode . . . to anticipate customer needs." Act II is seeking to be more prepared for new markets and products. The Internet has been implemented as an effective way to gauge customer needs. In addition, different media are being used to build Lowe's name and collect data. As an example, Lowe's has joined with the Home & Garden Network for advertising and exclusive sponsorship of shows and other cable networks and magazines.[8]

It goes without saying that information is power. As technology empowers individuals and companies to learn more about the world around them, there is a fear that privacy becomes compromised. From my experience, there are proper ways in which to acquire data about your customers and use the data in a respectful manner. Unfortunately, there are many instances when the information gathered is implemented in a tasteless manner. It has been reported that some supermarkets have gone so far as to target hapless customers whose partner or dog has just died.[9]

Databases should be used to track incentive points, needed ancillary products, and the communication frequency with the customer. The boundaries for the usage of the database should be driven by commonsense values and a high degree of sensitivity. Businesses should be sensitive to the needs of the customer. Further, do not overstay your welcome. Be sensitive to the contact window and the periodicity with which it is used. Also, be sensitive to the information you keep. Make sure it's only relevant to your business and doesn't compromise your company's integrity. Finally, be sensitive to the message you send. Remember, customers know you are gathering information on them. Don't overstep your bounds or you'll be sorry later.

SUMMARY

The most valuable customers—who will keep you in business and guarantee future profits—are those who buy from you again and again and again. Smart companies in the new millennium are those that do the following when it comes to building customer loyalty:

- Smart companies anticipate when and how a customer buys.

- Smart companies identify customers' shopping frequency.

- Smart companies build an accumulating incentive program that rewards the customer for frequent and multiple purchases rather than for a single transaction.

- Smart companies offer an ordering system tailored to the specific needs of the customer.

- Smart companies, where possible, create a consumable product with a "use-it-up" philosophy.

Three ways in which the smartest companies and individuals own the customer's buying cycle, or loop, are:

- Offering accumulative incentives with every purchase

- Effectively managing the after-purchase needs of the customer

- Proactively anticipating future purchases

CHAPTER 7

Educating the Customer

> *"Educated customers don't go away from great products regardless of the price."*
>
> —Thom Winninger

Today's customers actively seek to understand as much as to be understood. I call it the "know-a-bility" factor. However, information simply for the sake of information is not what drives smart companies to inform their customers about their products or services. I cannot begin to tell you the number of companies I see who put out a seemingly endless proliferation of confusing and often worthless information with the intent of educating their customers. Smart companies understand that know-a-bility is delivering the particular information that addresses your customers' specific needs.

As a manufacturer, I want to know how your specific process will integrate itself within my unique business process. As a homeowner, I want to know how your fireplace meets my distinct environmental needs. As a windsurfer, I want to know how your board approaches my own level of experience and desire for excitement rather than what it does for everyone. In the majority of cases, customers want to know as much about application of your product or service as specification. They want to understand as much about what the product or service does for them as what it is about.

Educating customers also means teaching them how to buy your product. I call this the "how-and-why-a-bility" aspect of the process. This is the point on which you want your customer to judge your product or service. Diamond wholesalers, for example, work to educate their customers on how to judge the quality of a diamond by using grade, color, and clarity. In this case, the industry has gone to the length of developing a grading system for diamonds and publishing it for public consumption. Accordingly, the how and why is not simply what the product does. It is an assessment of why your product or service is of value to the customer and how buying what you offer is the only real answer.

Boat buyers want to know how to judge performance and durability. Golfers want to understand how to judge a club's performance. Nonprofit donors want to know how to evaluate the impact of their contribution to the agency to which they are giving. Simply stated, the better you define the real and specific needs of your customers, the easier it will be to create an education strategy for them to judge you.

Educating your customers is a holistic effort. It must take into account the total approach in providing your customers the information they truly need. Smart companies capture their customers by implementing three proven strategies: (1) educating the customer about what the product or service does; (2) educating the customer about how to buy from you; and (3) educating the customer about the application of the customer's greatest need.

EDUCATING CUSTOMERS ABOUT WHAT THE PRODUCT OR SERVICE DOES

There is no doubt about the importance of informing your customers what your product or service can do for them. Basic statistics and facts are critical in answering the basic questions about your product or service. Nevertheless, such data are typically not the most important factors in the buying decision. Research continually shows that the more relevant the information is to customers' personal needs, the more likely they are to buy the product or service. Unfortunately, in terms of customer education, most companies spend the vast majority of their resources talking about the benefits of their product or service on a general and nonspecific level.

Relevancy to customers' needs must dictate the information given to customers about what the product or service does. It astounds me how many companies try to push their product onto a customer who could care less about benefits the company views as indispensable. Lawn mower manufacturers, for example, consistently harp on the turning radius of their mowers, while research shows a large percentage of American lawns don't even have obstructions worth the effort.

Smart companies are making efficient use of technology to educate their customers. The changing dynamics of knowledge acquisition is compelling companies to rethink the way information is presented to the marketplace. The proper application of information technology is an increasingly powerful tool successful firms use to address the needs of their customers.

First Union Corporation

First Union Corporation's overhaul of its consumer banking division has been a terrific success primarily because of the company's ability to properly educate its customers about what the bank does and can do. Instead of viewing its traditionally expensive branches as the center for transactions (e.g., deposits, withdrawals, loan applications, etc.), First Union attempted to turn branches into customer education centers. Every visit to a First Union branch is viewed by management as a way to teach customers about more convenient and cost-effective banking channels such as the Internet, ATMs, and call centers.

The experience has shown that when customers are fully informed about the security and convenience that comes with non-branch banking, they are more likely to stay customers and purchase other services. A further benefit is the reduced cost for the bank. Jack M. Antonini, executive vice president, reckons that transactions executed over the Internet cost 4 cents when development costs are factored out versus $3 in a branch. Says Antonini, "A better-educated customer is a more valuable and loyal one."

From the perspective of an automobile manufacturer, the dealership network makes up its customer base. Its consumer is the individual who purchases the vehicle. One of the strategies leading automotive companies use to meet these highest needs is educating their dealers about what their cars do. For companies like Porsche, Nissan, and Lexus, this means better educating their dealers about the products they are selling to the end users.

Porsche

Porsche Cars North America is encouraging its dealers to use the Internet as a way to improve the education of its customers. Porsche has put all of its training materials—videos, reference materials—on a dealer-only Web site. The Web site enables Porsche to communicate with its dealers, aka customers, in real time. In the past, dealers often consulted dated information, but the site offers a reference library, video collection, self-study courses, chat rooms, and links with Porsche employees. Porsche, who spent more than $500,000 on the Web site, sees the benefits in this way: A better-educated dealer (customer) can provide a higher rate of service and eventual return business.

Lexus

Innovative leaders like Lexus and Nissan are combining dealer education and consumer events into one, getting more bang for their marketing buck. Lexus has extended the reach of its Taste of Lexus series. The program attracts upscale buyers with gourmet food and test-drives during weekend sessions at local theme parks and event sites in Miami, New York, Washington, Chicago, Cleveland, Los Angeles, and San Francisco. Lexus has combined these events with a two-day dealer education program in which new technologies via the Internet and strategies like relationship marketing are discussed with dealers.

Nissan

Nissan has established a similar, if not quite as deluxe, educational program for its dealers. It has set up dealership training meetings in over 30 cities. Immediately after the training event, car buyers—the customers of Nissan—are invited to the venues to view and perhaps even test-drive vehicles.[1] In each case, the focus on the distinctive nature of each customer is well understood and respected. Further, the need to educate customers so they can properly inform the end user is explicit.

English Ideas

English Ideas, the makeup producer known for such products as Lip Last and Brow Enhance, has installed monitors that feature videotaped beauty advice at the touch of a screen to build excitement in stores and, more important, to educate customers with a consistent message. The computer program has four sections—Lips, Face, Brows, and Eyes—that feature advice and tips about various types of products. Another section, Beauty Tips, features beauty experts discussing grooming issues unrelated to English Ideas products. Customers just touch the screen to jump to a specific section. "Instead of wanting gift-with-purchase, consumers want straightforward information," says President and founder Rebecca Pfluegner.

Firstar Corporation

Firstar Corporation of Milwaukee, Wisconsin, a regional banking company, is claiming to receive tremendous benefits from its efforts to educate investors in its mutual funds. In shareholder statements, the company has been including lengthy discussions of the investment strategies, types of investments, principal volatility, and yield of its mutual funds. In addition, Firstar has been sending a quarterly newsletter, which deals with trends in the marketplace, to investors. "The better-informed and better-educated clients make better decisions," according to Mary Ellen Stanek, president of Firstar Investment Research and Management Company.

Johnston and Murphy

Andy Gilber, vice president of marketing for Nashville-based Johnston and Murphy, said educating customers about care for their footwear offers added value. Attached to every pair of Johnston and Murphy shoes is a card that details how to care for all the materials that comprise their products. "We prefer to help customers care for their shoes through education," said Gilbert. He noted that the information contributes to Johnston and Murphy's brand identity, and that the company isn't merely selling shoes but a lifestyle.[2]

Monetta Family of Mutual Funds

The Monetta Family of Mutual Funds, based in Wheaton, Illinois, is increasing the marketing of The Monetta Express Kids Investment Program. Under the program, children, in conjunction with their parents or grandparents, are encouraged to save for their needs.

The program, which maintains a minimum investment of $250, was designed to educate children about the benefits of mutual fund investing and at the same time make it fun for the kids. Lessons about investing are presented in a 16-page activity book that includes discussions about diversification, the differences between short-term and long-term needs, and a simplified discussion of risk along with pages to color and puzzles to solve.

Los Angeles Dodgers

To increase the number of games that children attend and to educate them about baseball, the Los Angeles Dodgers have created Kids' Clubhouse. The Dodgers believe the increasing amount of sports entertainment available is diluting the potential fan base of baseball. More children today play soccer than any other organized activity. To get kids into baseball, Kids' Clubhouse provides children with an inside look into America's pastime. Autograph sessions with players, on-field practices with coaches, and stadium tours provide kids with a much stronger understanding of the nuances of baseball.

Ramsey National Bank and Trust

Ramsey National Bank and Trust in Devils Lake, North Dakota, is recognized year after year as one of the best companies in America for educating its customers. According to Mike Connor, bank president, Ramsey makes a concerted effort to consistently educate citizens of all ages about managing money. The following are just some of the educational programs the bank offers the community:

- How to Do Your Banking. Ramsey partners with ninth-graders from Four Winds High School on the Spirit Lake Indian Reservation in nearby Fort Totten to teach them how checking accounts work. Part of the process involves children practicing to write checks. The banks how-to program—a seven-part enhanced program dealing with bank services—gives students a chance to analyze loan applications, calculate disposable income, and understand the complicated language of credit reports.
- Moola Moola and Money Minders/Pencil Pantry. Ramsey teams up with 550 elementary school students to teach them about saving money regularly through its Moola Moola program. The Pencil Pantry project puts students at

the head of a "company" and gives them tools to help them run their own business.

- Heritage Club. Ramsey works with senior citizen groups, holding monthly seminars throughout the community to provide investment and retirement planning advice. The bank also sends a monthly Heritage Club newsletter to seniors.

Dr. Scholl's

For the past three years, Dr. Scholl's has had two mobile foot care centers traveling across the country promoting foot health education and introducing the latest foot care devices. With a highly active but aging baby boom population, consumers are beginning to pay more attention to foot care. Still, these same people may be fully aware of the potential treatment or remedy options. Clover Bergmann, vice president of foot care marketing, says, "With eight out of ten people suffering some kind of foot problem during their lifetime, consumer interest in the tour is at an all time high." He adds, "A big part of the tour is a tie-in with our retail partners. Overall, the response from retailers has been very positive. We have the same goal as our trade partners do, which is to educate customers about the products that are available to them."[3]

EDUCATING CUSTOMERS ABOUT HOW TO BUY FROM YOU

Customers today are more inclined to buy from you if they are educated about how to do it. Airlines are educating customers on how to use e-ticket machines in airports. Amazon.com walks visitors to its Web site through a stress-free process of buying books. The floral industry, led by 1-800-FLOWERS, is teaching customers how to order flowers for anyone, from anywhere, to anywhere, 24 hours a day, 7 days a week.

Further, the use of information technology to educate your customers about how to buy from you is increasingly being used by leading companies as a successful and cost-effective way to maximize their value.

1800DAYTRADE.COM

The unprecedented growth in the stock market and the meteoric rise in the popularity of day trading on the Internet has led to astounding profits for several new firms. 1800DAYTRADE.COM, a Dallas-based online day trading firm, has launched live online videos and audio seminars to attract new customers and educate already active investors about the differences between Nasdaq Market Level II trading platforms. These platforms are directly linked to the markets that the firm offers. The live events are targeted toward active equity traders, who the firm defines as individuals who trade more than once a day. The seminars run from one to two hours and are designed to educate active traders on the advantages of using the firm's Level II trading platforms.

RML Trading

RML Trading, a Bellevue, Washington–based discount brokerage, is offering StockCam, an education program similar to 1800DAYTRADE.COM's. According to Linda Kendall, vice president of education, "The industry is failing to educate investors. Clients deserve options that help them to understand more about electronic trading." Kendall added that from a compliance standpoint, it makes sense for the firm to educate its investors so they don't blame the firm when they lose money.

Chat rooms, once viewed only as a seamy aspect of cyberspace, are now being moved into the mainstream by companies seeking ways to interact more intimately with their customers over the Internet. As a business tool, chat rooms hold the promise of real-time, live body feedback for customers who want immediate and specific information about the products and services they purchase. Further, chat rooms reduce a company's dependence on the telephone as a means of conducting customer education as well as the costly call centers and toll-free lines that go with it.[4]

Symantec

Symantec, a software company with about $500 million in annual sales, has employed about 500 people to handle thousands of calls a week at its customer service center in Eugene, Oregon. The company, which provides free education about its software for 90 days, has been encouraging customers to visit a chat room off their Web page.

Chase Manhattan Bank

Like Symantec, Chase Manhattan Bank is looking at chat rooms as a way to assist retail customers who run into difficulty while using its Web site. "Rather than have that customer walk away unsatisfied and without the information they need, we want to provide a safety valve where somebody from Chase can help that customer right away," says William Graham, Chase's manager of Internet services.[5]

Learnlots.com

With nearly 15 million people buying online for the first time every year, it is incumbent for Web retailers to educate their customers on how to buy from them. For many new buyers, Learnlots.com has become the educational source for preparing buyers with crucial online shopping tips. With Web stores expecting revenues of $12 billion in the 2000 holiday season, Learnlots.com is focusing on making the shopping experience of the Web a seamless experience.

Consumers who enjoy the convenience of shopping at home but are concerned about maintaining the same level of service they receive from a brick-and-mortar store can click on Learnlots.com, which emphasizes safe online shopping tips. Included in the Portal Shopping tutorial are helpful suggestions for navigating and controlling the virtual purchase process.

Learnlots.com provides its Web partners with thousands of tutorials covering a broad range of topics, including computer hardware and software, the Internet, consumer electronics, and lifestyles as well as many others. The company provides its tutorials free of charge to its partners as well as to its Web user partners. Learnlots.com generates revenue from advertising, e-commerce activity, and commissions earned each time a consumer clicks through and purchases products related to the tutorials.

"The Internet is changing the way consumers buy airline tickets, toys, computers, and clothes. Our goal with this tutorial is to provide a smarter approach to buying on the Web," says Mark Thompson, chief executive officer of Learnlots.com.[6]

Espanol.com

Espanol.com, the first large-scale online retailer for Spanish speakers, created an automated, bilingual customer service designed to enhance and simplify e-shoppers' experience at its Web site. "Espanol.com recognizes that customer education and service is an area where we can build a niche for ourselves in this crowded marketplace," says Kyle McNamara, president and CEO of Espanol. com. "For Espanol.com's users, top-notch service and education are more than just a Spanish-speaking operator. Latino shoppers want someone who can understand their shopping needs and instantly respond to their requests. With only a handful of sites realizing this, Espanol.com is positioned to become the preferred online superstore for consumers who want exclusive and hard-to-find Latin products."

The first Spanish-language Internet site certified by the better business bureau, Espanol.com features a broad selection of books, music, and videos as well as exclusive and hard-to-find merchandise. Staffed by highly trained bilingual and bicultural professionals, the

Instant Response Center consists of a complete Web and telephony-based solution that provides customer education, up-to-the-minute information on order status and sales inquiries, and personalized product recommendations along with technical and navigational assistance.

Espanol.com educates its customers by relying on three features to simplify Latino shoppers' online experience and provide the highest quality of customer service options available on the Net today:

1. Online chat: Provides uninterrupted responses to customer service inquiries for those who require the immediate attention of a bilingual and bicultural professional.
2. E-mail: Guarantees a response to 80 percent of customer e-mails in less than 3 hours and the remaining 20 percent in 24 hours for those who don't require instant attention.
3. Toll-free telephone: Provides direct access to live, bilingual operators within seconds for those needing to hear a reassuring voice.

EDUCATING CUSTOMERS ABOUT THE APPLICATION OF THEIR HIGHEST NEED

My wife and I recently remodeled our kitchen. Although almost anyone who has attempted to choose new flooring, wall covering, appliances, and colors will admit it is a frustrating process, our experience was made much easier by our personal kitchen designer. From the first day until the end, we were daily asked a series of application-oriented questions intended to define our parameters of the multiple choices available. The kitchen designer, through probing and asking insightful questions, gleaned our highest need and built her service around it—and in the process creating maximum value for herself. Smart companies are those that don't simply educate their customers but also tailor their process to the application of their customers' highest need.

Pacific Gas and Electric Company (PG&E), California's leading supplier of gas and electricity, realized the highest educational need of its customers was to help them better manage their gas and electric usage. Research showed a large percentage of their customers were clueless when it came to understanding the role of energy in their life. As a result, PG&E has launched a series of two-month educational efforts to help customers better manage their gas and electric bills. Beverly Alexander, PG&E's vice president, said, "Our goal is to give people the information they need to evaluate their energy needs and usage." Through the series, the company informs customers of ways to manage their energy costs, including learning how to break down where their energy dollars go, how to choose energy-efficient appliances for their homes, and how to stay cooler during summer heat waves. "We have designed this educational series in response to the most frequently asked questions from our customers," said Alexander. "We trust people will take advantage of the information and, as always, we value our customers' input, which was received via e-mail, surveys, or through our Smarter Energy Line."[7]

The role of information technology as an element in the process of educating customers about the application of their highest need is becoming increasingly relevant. Manufacturers often give CD-ROMs to their customers as a way to display their products and order them online. One such company that is doing just that is Red Wing Shoe. A highly respected work and sports boot producer for decades, the company recently opened a store in the Mall of America in Minneapolis to educate and ultimately convert shoppers to its line of products.

On entering the store, shoppers encounter an interpretive center designed specifically to educate casual shoppers in the nation's largest mall about the company's history, products, and manufacturing process primarily through photos, videos, and CD-ROMs.[8]

SUMMARY

Today's customers actively seek to understand as much as to be understood. I call it the know-a-bility factor. However, information simply for the sake of information is not what drives smart companies to inform their customers about their products or services. Educating your customer is a holistic effort. It must take into account the total approach in providing your customers the information they truly need. Smart companies capture their customers by implementing three proven strategies:

- Educating customers about what the product or service does

- Educating customers about how to buy from you

- Educating customers about the application of their highest need

CHAPTER 8

Identifying Your Destination

"Without a destination, your company becomes tactically unsuccessful rather than strategically dominant."

—Thom Winninger

It may appear harsh, but companies that will thrive in the new millennium are those that are able to cope with constant change and foster their own and others' creativity. The attribute that will contribute most to your company's success will not simply be its technological skills. The language and tools that allow access to the digital world are always evolving, and there isn't a person alive who knows where it is heading. Instead, it will be the ability of your company to look at the big picture and adapt your mind-set to a new world where achievement will be measured not by usage of the firm's assets but rather by mind and creativity control. In other words, competitive advantage will go to those companies that possess the intellectual and creative capacity to fully grasp the changing nature of the structure of their market. The winners will be those companies that, having learned this, determine where their lucrative market niche lies.

The digital revolution and specifically the Internet have changed forever the idea that bigger is better. Amazon.com, founded just five years ago, is now worth over $20 billion with more than 5 million online customers. Dell Computers sells over $7 billion worth of computer hardware online. Cisco Systems, which didn't exist until about ten years ago, has a greater capitalization rate than such traditional corporate giants as Ford and General Motors.

Information technology and the Internet put power and choice back in the hands of the consumer, negating the often monopolistic market control strategy of many companies. Product search engines now filter the World Wide Web to find the best deals regardless of country, brand, or company.

The Internet revolution will take no prisoners. The winners may very well be new-style boutique businesses, which are faster, leaner, and altogether more adaptable than their peers, while today's established businesses with their successful strategies tailored to the world as it was are most likely to be at risk. This is not because established businesses can't change, but because the entrenched view at the top believes there is no need to.

Unfortunately, for too many companies senior management levels are the most likely places to find people with the least diversity of experience and the greatest reverence for the past. These individuals are the least likely to be living close to the future and the most likely to be farthest from the customer.

To prosper in the era of postindustrialization, a new mind-set and revolution within corporate culture are fundamental. Microsoft is a company on the edge of the daily transformation, where over 8,500 employees work in research and development with the goal of not only seeing the future but also creating it. It is a company led by Chairman Bill Gates that has identified its destination as always wanting to lead the race for the future.

Throughout time, individuals like Gates have changed the world with their vision of where they wanted to go and how to get there. The Wright brothers always wanted to fly, so they invented the airplane. Thomas Edison wanted to light his children's bedrooms at night, so he invented the light bulb. James Hill wanted settlers to move to the American Northwest, so he built a railroad.

In this ever more rapid age of disruptive and integrative technologies, it is crucial for your company to know: What is your destination? What are the changing opportunities? What technologies will sustain your success and market dominance? And what technologies will disrupt your success? A company without a destination will be unable to clearly survey the landscape and understand what the technological revolution means to the company. Without a strong sense of direction, a wandering company will look at the tactical, rather than strategic, level of technology—like a golf course without greens.

To effect a destination that captures and supports the dominance of your product or service, your company must address three crucial components: (1) the changing profile and needs of your customer universe; (2) the competitive universe in which your customer shops for and buys your product or service; and (3) the specific technologies and their rate of effectiveness that provide an ability to sell to that customer universe.

THE CHANGING PROFILE AND NEEDS OF YOUR CUSTOMER UNIVERSE

Fluidity within the marketplace is a reality of our age. The profile and needs of your customer are always changing. Success or failure in the new economy is increasingly resting on the ability of companies to shape a destination that agrees with the inevitable shifts in their customer universe.

Comcast Corporation

Comcast Corporation's sales group identified its most important goal as the conversion of advertisers to the benefits of cable television as a powerful way to get its message out. To accomplish this objective, Comcast realized it had to establish a strong salesforce in the field that was trained in the most current technology. Such a salesforce would only be possible, however, if an outstanding sales management team was in position. Comcast created a sales management internship for individuals it had identified as good candidates for sales manager positions. By knowing where it was going, Comcast could then formulate its strategies to achieve the objective of building a successful sales team.

A case of a company failing to adjust to the changes in its customer universe is illustrated in the following. In the first three quarters of 1998, a large Canadian mobile phone network had acquired 340,700 customers at an average cost of about $400. Not too bad. Almost immediately afterward, however, 259,600 walked out the door. Research revealed that over two-thirds of the defectors left because of a lack of perceived need for the service. They'd signed up primarily because of a free phone offer, low monthly service fees, and free airtime in the evening and on weekends. Moreover, very few of these customers stuck around long enough to pay back the cost of acquiring them. By failing to understand the highest needs of their changing customer universe, the Canadian company was forced to revamp its approach after losing millions of dollars and opportunity costs.

Bank One

In mid-1999 Bank One, a Chicago-headquartered lender doing business throughout the Midwest, wanted to do more business with middle-market companies, which are beginning to venture into foreign markets. Bank One International Corporation President D. P. Narayana stated the goal when he said, "If you look at trade statistics, the largest growth in export trade is coming from small to midsized companies—they are experiencing much faster export growth than larger U.S. corporations, which tend to have already penetrated the overseas market. Targeting this market is key to the international strategy of Bank One."[1]

Avon

Avon developed a long-term plan by calling itself "The Company for Women" prior to launching its first global ad campaign. Overall, the company's destination is to become one of the world's top-three beauty brands; it now ranks sixth, according to Avon executives. The development strategies toward its goal include increased ad spending; opening a retail store, salon, and spa in New York; and setting up 60 kiosks in shopping malls. The company is also considering more franchising, based on its successful test run in Malaysia.

Merck & Company

Merck & Company has sought to maintain its leading position in the global pharmaceutical market by developing an identity as a manufacturer of preventive medicines. To encourage prevention, the company has increased awareness of diseases for which specific remedies are lacking.

Merck's strategy allowed Singulair, a once-daily tablet for asthma, to become the market leader in its class within its introductory year. Maxalt and Maxalt-MLT, both for the treatment of migraine headaches, are marketed in 11 countries where they lead the market share for prevention of this common ailment. Propecia, the first and currently only tablet for the treatment of male pattern baldness, has experienced similar success.[2]

American Express

American Express Chairman and CEO Harvey Golub explains the company's vision for the future: First, to build and capitalize on the American Express brand name. According to Golub, "The implication of our brand strategy is that the name will be applied to products and services we offer when those products and services are critical to the brand positioning—it will not be used when the products are not critical to the brand.

"Second, to focus on serving individuals directly or through intermediaries. For example, in our sense the corporate card is a corporate business, but the consumer is the ultimate customer. The same is true for our 401(k) and retirement services business; we serve the corporation to reach the ultimate consumer."

Third, says Golub, is to work with and through partnerships. "This reflects a very substantial change in the company. Historically, we have been an organization that was vertically integrated. We manufactured everything that we sold. We serviced every product we manufactured. And now, we also partner." Such a strong statement regarding the company's destination from the chairman and CEO provides American Express with an identity about where it is headed.[3]

DuPont

DuPont, the Wilmington, Delaware–based company, has recently replaced its tag line after more than 65 years. The Better Things for Better Living tag line has been replaced by The Miracles of Science. The slogan was designed to reflect DuPont's change in its corporate destination as it seeks to be known as a leading technology company. "Clearly, we do not want to be seen as a chemical company," explained Kathleen Forte, VP of global corporate affairs. "It's really limiting, and it doesn't describe what we're about."

Some managers feared that the use of the word *Miracles* might seem hokey and perhaps unbelievable. But research within the company has indicated that employees on the whole have agreed with the concept. Said one North American employee, "The new destination has done a good job of tying together all of DuPont's businesses." A South American employee added, "It's absolutely related to DuPont, because we really do operate miracles through research." Carol Gee, corporate brand manager, confirmed the effective identification of the company's destination when she said, "There are no greater skeptics than a bunch of DuPont scientists and engineers. Hype is not something they buy into."[4]

THE COMPETITIVE UNIVERSE IN WHICH YOUR CUSTOMER SHOPS FOR AND BUYS YOUR PRODUCT OR SERVICE

Information technology has allowed businesses to streamline their operations and deal with their customers in ways not even imagined just a few years ago. Retailers can monitor sales at the checkout counter and restock their shelves even before a popular product is sold out. Wal-Mart records every sale in every one of its stores in a giant data warehouse. The company uses the data to fashion targeted marketing strategies while distributing products to the stores where the most people are likely to buy them.

Leading companies understood early on that the revolution in information technology was dramatically changing the universe in which their customers shopped or bought their products and services. In the process, these companies have altered the terms and engagement of their industries. Companies like General Electric and Federal Express have changed the economics of their basic businesses by offering services that are possible because of electronic commerce.

General Electric conducts portions of its supplier bidding online, lowering acquisition costs and increasing competition among suppliers while limiting the bureaucracy of the bid process. Federal Express leverages its package handling by having customers perform their own inquiries on the status of shipments. Such integration with technology provides greater customer control and convenience at a lower cost.

Ticketmaster

Ticketmaster, the nation's leading event ticketing agency, has brought new meaning to the question, "May I show you to your seats?" As part of a technology strategy that the company describes as a cornerstone of its effort to enhance its future growth, Ticketmaster's Web site allows customers to view their seats and take a three-dimensional fly-through of the concert hall or arena. With these new features, Ticketmaster is attracting new customers by turning electronic ticket buying into an entertainment experience itself.

QuikOrder, Inc.

QuikOrder, Inc., is one of those companies that truly understands the competitive nature of its customer universe. In 1998, for the first time in American history, more money was spent at restaurants than at grocery stores and food marts combined. In short, Americans are cooking at home less and less. As a result, the Chicago-based home delivery service expanded to the Internet and now enables customers to use the Web to place home delivery or carryout orders from participating restaurants by accessing the QuikOrder.com site.

After customers connect to QuikOrder.com, they enter their delivery address and the QuikOrder service automatically determines the stores that serve them. If choosing a pizza, for example, from Domino's, consumers can choose the size of the pizza and the ingredients they want as well as side orders and beverages. Once the order entry is completed, it is transmitted to QuikOrder's server, which in turn sends it to the participating store closest to the customer. This process takes just seconds and the store then sends an e-mail confirmation to the customer with the estimated delivery time based on real-time store statistics. Ray Anderson, president of QuikOrder.com, speaks of his company's destination when he says, "Our experience has documented our long-held belief that QuikOrder.com offers great convenience for customers and provides restaurants with a powerful, highly flexible marketing and customer service tool."[5]

Applied Industrial Technologies

Applied Industrial Technologies, Inc., of Cleveland, Ohio, and National Semiconductor Corporation of Santa Clara, California, are business-to-business companies that share one thing in common: they have both embarked on e-commerce to enhance customer loyalty, boost sales, and cut operating costs.

Applied is a distributor that carries over 1.5 million products from different manufacturers. To simplify the buying process for its customers, the distributor decided to provide them access to a private extranet where they can view the products it sells along with their prices. Applied's Web site also enables customers to buy products online, check real-time inventory of its different branches, and view their orders from the past two years.

National Semiconductor Corporation

Unlike other companies, National has two Web sites. The purpose is to cater to its two types of customers: those whose accounts are handled by its direct salesforce and those handled by its distributor network. Both of National's e-commerce Web sites were designed to streamline the sales process and provide services to customers that are impossible to provide offline.

National's e-commerce Web site for its customers who buy from its direct salesforce is basically a customer service tool. Each customer is assigned a private extranet that can be used to look at product specifications, verify order status, and view order history. Because most customers purchase through electronic data interchange (EDI), they cannot use the e-commerce Web site as a buying tool.

On the other hand, the e-commerce Web site that National created for its customers who buy through its distributor is an open site. This means that customers can not only use it to buy products but also to coordinate their purchases and determine which distributor they buy from.

Sabre Inc.

Recognizing the highly competitive environment in which travel agencies must now operate, Sabre recently delivered a suite of solutions that capitalize on the power of the Internet to assist travel agencies by increasing revenue, lowering operating costs, and providing greater value to its clients. (Operating as The SABRE Group Holdings, the company became Sabre Inc. in 1999.)

Sabre, one of the leaders in applying information technology to meet the needs of the travel and transportation industries, realized Internet and Web technologies were dramatically altering the needs of its customer universe. With the creation of a new personalized Web page, each of Sabre's connected agents can provide travel-booking services to its customers via the Web while integrating bookings with the traveler's information in the Sabre system. Agencies also receive a free listing in the Travelocity.com agency directory, providing access to more than seven million online users. "Our strategy is to leverage the Internet and new technologies to provide e-commerce tools to Sabre-connected agencies," said Sam Gilliand, senior vice president of product marketing for Sabre. "This reinforces our commitment to providing travel agents with innovative technology and real cost savings."

Sabre also offers a variety of information about delivery options that provide agencies with the flexibility to balance business requirements with cost and optimize the choice of network connectivity for main offices, branches, and remote users. The ability of SABRE to harness the Internet and new technologies is becoming critical in helping many travel agents provide unparalleled service to their clients. Sami Jabri of Travel the World Services, Inc., in New York, speaks for thousands of Sabre's clients when he says, "With seamless updates and technology enhancements, Sabre provides tools that are essential to running my business."[6]

Dell Computer

Dell Computer, mentioned here earlier, may be one of the purest examples of how a company can flourish by understanding its competitive universe. Unlike its floundering main competitor Compaq, which uses a vast and costly network of resellers, Dell sells all of its systems directly to its customers. The company waits until it has received an order before it begins to build a machine. "We don't have to guess what our customers are going to buy," says Michael Dell, the company's founder and chairman. "They tell us every day."[7]

THE SPECIFIC TECHNOLOGIES
AND THEIR RATE OF EFFECTIVENESS
PROVIDING ACCESS TO
YOUR CUSTOMER UNIVERSE

Electronic commerce has become the great geographic equalizer, allowing businesses with no physical presence in a particular market to compete with the locals on a near-equal footing. Companies like Charles Schwab and Fidelity were among the pioneers in using telephones, computers, and customer databases to provide prompt, personalized service, often at a distance. But that is only part of the story.

These companies understood electronic commerce before many others caught on. They realized financial products are largely commodities, differentiated in customers' eyes by accompanying services. Both Schwab and Fidelity built their organizations around these value propositions, which resulted in a business model that is driving in a new culture, enabled by new technology and focused on meeting customer needs.[8] For Schwab, this translates into more than $75 billion in online assets and nearly one million active online accounts. For Fidelity, it means a wide range of services, enhanced profitability, and the ability to offer trades at low commissions.

Although the explosion of retail Web sites selling books, music, airline tickets, and computer equipment seem to always be in the news, many analysts believe the Internet quite possibly offers the richest potential for growth as a business-to-business medium. According to Stan Dolberg, director of software strategies at Forrester Research in Cambridge, Massachusetts, "Business-to-business commerce is really where the big growth on the Internet is." In many cases, business-to-business commerce involves existing relationships between companies—and does not require the fundamental changes in buying habits that mark online consumer retail. Dolberg adds, "It's a much smaller leap. It's their lifeblood for these people to do business with each other."

Sajar Plastics

Joseph Bergen, president of Sajar Plastics, a $15 million plastic-parts maker in Middlefield, Ohio, said he landed a $150,000 order for injection molds from a machine-building company in upstate New York as a result of participating in Polysort, a Web marketplace for the plastics and rubber industries launched in neighboring Akron. "It was an honest-to-goodness lead out of the clear blue sky," said Bergen, who pays Polysort less than $2,000 a year to design and host his company's Web site. "You have to be crazy not to spend the money!"[9]

Industry.net

Industry.net covers the vast industrial manufacturing market. Claiming to be the biggest business-to-business Web marketplace, Industry.net counts among its members 300,000 purchasing agents from large and midsized manufacturers and distributors and about 4,500 sellers. Robert Kraisner, president of Strong Toll Company, a $60 million regional distributor of supplies to the automotive and steel industries, said he won his first overseas contract through Industry.net: a $60,000 order for abrasives from a steel manufacturer in Indonesia. "The market today is becoming more dispersed, and it's very hard to stay on top of it," said Kraisner, who pays about $30,000 a year so Industry.net will showcase his Cleveland firm. "It's the difference between a few customers and many."[10]

Toyota

Toyota is now selling auto service and repair manuals on the Internet as part of a business-to-business e-commerce initiative aimed to support its customers—Toyota dealers. Toyota plans to expand the program to sell other products and services in the future. Gordon Moog, manager of Toyota Motor Sales, USA, wholesale programs and dealer communications, says, "Toyota recognizes the value of the Internet as a vehicle to grow business-to-business sales." Tom Zawacki, vice president of Modern Media, a leading builder and marketer of e-business services says, "Providing customers a personalized Internet experience, combined with the ability to easily purchase products and services online, will help Toyota provide an unmatched level of Internet customer service found today in the automobile industry." [11]

Autobytel.com

Autobytel.com is the leading international company of online automotive e-commerce. Year 2000 sales are expected to exceed more than $1.2 billion per month through its Accredited Dealer Network. Widely held as the most comprehensive automotive Internet site, Autobytel.com offers consumers a positive purchasing and ownership experience while providing its dealer network with the most efficient way to reach online buyers. According to Mark Lorimer, president and CEO, "We have set the benchmark for the automotive e-commerce segment. Our U.S. operations alone generate more than $1.6 million an hour—24/7—in car sales through our network of dealers." He also pointed out that Autobytel.com sells more cars than its two closest competitors combined. In addition, Autobytel.com is the eighth most recognized e-commerce brand and the first most recognized brand in the online car-buying space, according to Opinion Research Corporation.

In the hypercompetitive mortgage lending industry, smart lenders are taking to the Web as a way to have better access to their customer universe. According to Nick Karris, senior analyst at Gomez Advisors, the Internet's premiere rating service, "The online mortgage market shows great promise for continued growth because consumers have easy access to information and approvals. Customers can close faster online and, most important, they can save as much as $2,000 from online lenders because they offer lower rates and closing costs." [12]

According to Karris, online mortgage sites attract three types of customers: rate hunters, who look for immediate quotes, instant approvals, and low rates; one-stop home shoppers, who want basic services and ancillary offerings; and novice buyers, who demand demos, mortgage calculators, educational content, and outstanding customer service. [13] Successful mortgage lenders, like businesspeople in other industries, will be the ones who identify the changes within their customer universe and direct the appropriate technology toward them.

SUMMARY

It may appear harsh, but the companies that will thrive in the new millennium are those that can cope with constant change and foster their own and others' creativity. It will be the ability of your company to look at the big picture and adapt your mind-set to a new world where achievement will be measured not by usage of the firm's assets but rather by mind and creativity control.

To effect a destination that captures and supports the dominance of your product and service, your company must address the three crucial components:

- The changing profile and needs of your customer universe

- The competitive universe in which your customer shops for and buys your product or service

- The specific technologies and their rate of effectiveness providing you access to your customer universe

CHAPTER 9

Promoting Differences

"A nose of a difference in a horse race makes for a whole horse of a difference in the winning of the race."

—Thom Winninger

To be a leading company, it is fundamental to effectively present the differences between the competition and your product or service. In order to come closer to the goal of attaining full price, companies need to benchmark the uniqueness of what they are and build upon the differences they possess.

Nevertheless, in too many situations, companies are unable to identify any real differences between themselves and the competition. How much time is it said in meeting rooms across North America: "We have the greatest people" or "Nobody beats us on service."

Traditionally, hardware stores, like dozens of other retailers, have kept customers coming back by offering good prices, quality merchandise, and great service. "But everything is different these days," says Mike Morris, owner of Morris Home Hardware in Ottawa. As a third-generation owner of a 3,500-square-foot store in operation since 1947, Morris believes the big boys have changed the notion of repeat business. "Customer service isn't necessarily enough anymore when you've got three Home Depots in town."[1] Unfortunately, if customers are unable to adequately differentiate your product or service from the competition, the only way to set yourself apart is to cut the price. And if your competition is like Home Depot, you are going to have a lot of problems.

Simply put, companies that effectively differentiate their product or service are the ones that hold a competitive advantage over their rivals. Smart companies are those that invest the necessary thought, work, and attention needed to correctly identify, demonstrate, and communicate their differences in terms of the premium customer profile.

IDENTIFY YOUR DIFFERENCES

In my experience in working with Wells' Blue Bunny Ice Cream, we together identified that there was a strong need to accentuate the special qualities of its branded product to its customer—the retail grocer. After strategizing with Wells' management, we were able to create a program that promoted the differences of the ice cream and justified the claims about high quality. The outcome of this focus on differentiation was an increased market share at the retail level and higher margins.

Thomas College

Thomas College, a small private business college in Waterville, Maine, has seen a large increase in its enrollment by differentiating itself from other institutions by guaranteeing job placement to its graduates. It isn't another gimmick. A student must earn a minimum 2.75 cumulative GPA from a baccalaureate degree program at Thomas College and successfully complete either an internship or a cooperative work experience. In effect, the college has defined and differentiated itself from the competition by concentrating on a very specific objective. Although assuring students of a job after graduation puts the college on the line, it provides prospective students and their parents with a unique reason for looking at Thomas College.

Toys "R" Us

For Toys "R" Us, the differentiation between themselves and their competition has been the chain's ability to look for goods that separate them from their competitors. According to Michael Goldstein, vice chairman and CEO, "We keep trying to differentiate"; although he notes that it is increasingly difficult to do so in a sea of popular name brand toys that all toy retailers must offer.

As a result, in 1999, Toys "R" Us launched its own line of toys called Geoffrey's World that caters to infants and toddlers. Also, it is actively seeking exclusive merchandise arrangements with its vendors. By trying to create a unique selection of merchandise, Toys "R" Us is identifying its differences from the competition.

Kayne Anderson Investment Management

Kayne Anderson Investment Management, a West Coast–based acquisition group, recently purchased two small, but well-established, niche bakeries—Miss Grace's Lemon Cakes and Mrs. Beasley's. When Kenneth Harris, former president and CEO of W. R. Restaurant Group, was put in charge, he immediately saw an opportunity to differentiate the local bakeries and create a national presence.

Harris saw the Internet as a way to merge the retail operations and product lines and build a new business into a national supplier of high-end corporate gifts. Says Harris, "We looked around and realized that nobody had a Web site that catered to business gift giving, so we decided to build a site that would enable a business to go online and send gifts to 300 or 400 people."

The first step toward differentiation from other mom and pop bakeries was to put up a modest Web site with the capacity to take orders online. Later, a multiple-recipient module was created to provide corporate customers with their own personal password–protected accounts that show them to whom they gave gifts last year and let them decide to whom they want to send gifts this year. Customers can go to their account and edit their lists, change them, save them, and come back whenever they're ready to finalize their orders. Adds Harris, "The identification of this capability has completely differentiated us in the marketplace. Most important, it's already profitable."[2]

DEMONSTRATE YOUR DIFFERENCES

Once a company has identified the unique and different aspects of its product or service, it needs to demonstrate those differences to its customers.

Ritzman Pharmacies

Ritzman Pharmacies, a small eight-store chain operating within a 35-mile radius of Akron, Ohio, has historically promoted its differences to achieve success in the always competitive drugstore industry. Founded in 1950, the chain has been a leader in the creation and implementation of new strategies to set itself apart from the competition. According to Larry Fligor, vice president of sales and marketing and one of five pharmacists who now owns the company, the strategy of today focuses on standing apart in its market.

Rather than being simply another drugstore, Ritzman has positioned and differentiated itself as a health care destination. Its standard format measures 5,000 square feet, although one store—the Wadsworth, Ohio, location—breaks the mold at about 9,000 square feet. In its new stores, including the Wadsworth store, the chain has invested in a look that builds on its identity as a health care provider. Wood accents on shelving, low fixtures, and carpets all combine to give the stores a warm, comfortable look and set it apart from the drug mart look of some of its keenest competitors.

"Our stores are more expensive to set up, but it's part of our whole offering to look and be different than what a standard chain would look like," Fligor said. For example, juice bars featuring smoothie-type natural drinks are used to attract attention for the chain. Expanded vitamin lines similar to those sold in health food stores, freezers stocked with natural foods, and standardized herbs— including Ritzman's own private label offerings—line the shelves. Concluded Folger, "Other chains offer what they offer, but our confidence for the future comes from knowing there are enough people who are interested in our different type of pharmacy."[3]

First Tennessee Bank

First Tennessee Bank determined in 1995 that private-dial telephone options—although the newest attempt at personal banking—were not the wave of the future as most others in the banking industry thought. While the vast majority of their competitors were focusing on 1-800 private banking services, First Tennessee decided it needed to differentiate itself by offering a robust Internet service. So early in the consumer Internet revolution, First Tennessee was one of the first banks in the country to provide its customers with a more interactive, personalized service that could be more easily controlled than the 1-800 numbers. While other banks were testing the Web by building informational Internet sites, First Tennessee jumped in head first with a fully transactional, interactive offering branded FTB Online.

Senior management at First Tennessee was driven by the need to demonstrate its difference to the marketplace and take a giant leap ahead of the competition. This meant finding a Web banking solution that not only offered a rich, visually unique customer interface but would also enable First Tennessee to offer a wide array of personalized transactional services.

FTB Online went live in May 1998. At initial launch, FTB Online already had more than 600 customers who had signed up in advance and were waiting for the new system. That summer (1998), First Tennessee conducted a series of focus groups with customers to gauge first impressions. Customers responded very positively and especially responded well to the ATM Online, a friendly and familiar ATM interface displayed on the customer's PC that offered easy access to accounts.

At last count, FTB Online has more than 4,000 users, and applications are pouring into the bank. Moreover, 22 percent of new Internet customers are entirely new customers for the bank. And more than 90 percent of these new customers cite the availability of Internet banking as the major reason for joining up with First Tennessee.

A more important benefit for First Tennessee in its differentiation strategy has been the types of customers it has been attracting. Not only are they acquiring new customers through Internet banking, First Tennessee is also attracting the most desirable ones. Says Susan Terry, senior vice president for FTB Online, "Our studies show that Internet banking customers are twice as profitable as non-Internet customers. The Internet creates an instant demographic distinction: those who own a PC and have knowledge of the Internet are predominantly young and relatively affluent. These customers represent the 'emerging affluent' sector that constitutes the prime target of so many financial institutions."[4]

HOWS Markets

To compete with huge discounters such as Wal-Mart and Costco, which have been making inroads into grocery territory, small, entrepreneurial store operators are seeing the opportunity to demonstrate their differences in the marketplace. HOWS Markets, a new chain in southern California, has resurrected services abandoned years ago by other chains, such as home delivery, free knife sharpening, and an on-site butcher. HOWS stores are smaller—averaging between 20,000 to 40,000 square feet—around the fresh food departments at the perimeter of the store, leaving room at the center for primarily top name brand items. Because the stores are smaller and can tailor more of their stock to neighborhood tastes, HOWS is sure its customers won't complain about a slimmer selection of some popular items. Mark Oerum, one of the four partners in the new chain, explains it this way: "Everyone can sell the same can of Del Monte corn. But when it gets to differences in the meat, deli, produce, and bakery, that's where we make our statement."[5]

Farmer Jack Supermarkets

Like HOWS, Farmer Jack Supermarkets have not merely survived but have excelled against the big boys like Wal-Mart. As the leader in the Detroit metropolitan area for more than four decades, Farmer Jack has effectively differentiated itself from the competition. At the core, convenience has always been the overriding difference between Farmer Jack and all other Detroit-area markets. Farmer Jack was one of the first chains in the country to offer a café, freshly made meals-to-go, and other convenient services like a post office and pharmacy plus free membership and automatic savings in Farmer Jack's exclusive Bonus Savings Club and Baby Bonus Savings Club.[6]

COMMUNICATE YOUR DIFFERENCES

As I discussed earlier, leading companies focus on what the product will do for their customer at the premium level instead of merely touting what the product is. Moreover, leaders effectively communicate what those differences are.

Shell

Shell, for example, has successfully positioned itself as a supplier of convenience rather than a producer of high-quality gasoline. As recently as five years ago, oil companies like Shell foolishly focused on their octane ratings as the way to demonstrate what their product does. Unfortunately for most buyers of gasoline, high octane ratings sounded impressive but meant nothing to them.

What the oil industry had failed to understand was that their best customers couldn't care less about octane. Instead, what the customers really wanted was a quick, unimpeded way to fill up their tank at a self-serve pump. Shell learned this lesson and refocused its marketing efforts toward the creation of a perception of convenience. Its slogan "Moving at the speed of life" highlighted Shell's ability to get somebody a tank of gas in the shortest time possible. By communicating its differences, Shell was able to demonstrate how it was set apart from the rest of the competition.

Travelfest

With the airlines slashing the commissions paid to travel agents, one might wonder how anybody could survive in such a cutthroat environment. With such ticket-buying sites like Priceline.com and Travelocity.com stealing tens of thousands of customers away every day with cut-rate fares, is it possible that the travel agency might become a dinosaur in the near future? Possibly. But hold on. There is hope. There are agencies that are not only surviving but prospering nicely in this seemingly uninhabitable industry.

Travelfest in Austin, Texas, has succeeded where many have failed because it has communicated its differences effectively to the marketplace. Gary Hoover, president of the two-store agency, says the travel business has nearly missed the revolution in retail over the past 20 to 30 years. Most agencies close at 6 PM. They're not open on weekends, though their ads typically run on Sundays. Their offices are drab and uninviting. They do most of their business over the phone rather than face-to-face.

Hoover's stores are the antithesis of the industry. Walk into one of Travelfest's stores and you'll immediately realize you are in a very different environment. Fourteen video monitors are going at once. Four backlighted walls show slides from different parts of the world. The light fixtures are globes, the ceiling a giant mural.

The stores also sell some 20,000 travel-related items: books, videos, maps, luggage, water purifiers. Customers can pick up visa applications or check out the hotel and airline guides while their kids play in the Geofun learning center that offers 20 classes a month on travel-related subjects, from Spanish to how to overcome the fear of flying. Moreover, the store is open from 9 AM to 11 PM seven days a week. In an industry where most agencies are worried about making the payroll because of lower commissions, Travelfest is leading the way by differentiating itself and getting full price.[7]

SUMMARY

To be a leading company, it is fundamental to effectively present the differences between the competition and your product or service. In order to come closer to the goal of attaining full price, companies need to benchmark the uniqueness of what they are and build upon the differences they possess.

Smart companies are those that invest the necessary thought, work, and attention needed to correctly identify, demonstrate, and communicate their differences in terms of the premium customer profile.

CHAPTER 10

Substantiating Value, Not Price

"Value, not price, is the true authority in every marketplace."

—Thom Winninger

It is strikingly clear that economic control is moving rapidly away from producers and manufacturers while at the same time getting ever closer to consumers. Throughout most of its existence, capitalism has been predicated on the ability to overcome the scarcity of resources. In this environment, demand exceeded supply, and the elements of production—raw materials, land, and capital—were always scarce. In such a world, producers and manufacturers inevitably held the upper hand. However, over the past two decades, strong, undeniable forces have wrested control away from the traditional sources of economic power and increasingly placed authority in the hands of consumers.

Information technology, globalization, telecommunications, and deregulation have all contributed to the rise of a knowledge-based economy in which the old rules of traditional market economies no longer apply. Unlike real estate or petroleum, the conventional staples of the past model, knowledge is not scarce. Moreover, the abundance of knowledge makes it difficult for control to rest in the hands of a few individuals or companies. With knowledge now serving as the primary instrument of economic power, the limits of wealth creation seem limitless. Further, the physical and natural boundaries that formerly limited the building of wealth have become irrelevant. This dramatic shift from a resource-dependent economy to a knowledge-driven one is what has led to the ascendancy of the consumer.[1]

Time and time again we hear about the difficulty companies have in raising their prices much beyond the annual inflation rate, even as their level of service and quality improve. In addition, many companies find that their innovations are quickly replicated by their competitors and often improved. This "commoditization" of products and services tends to keep prices stagnant. As a result, profits need to originate from somewhere else. Increasingly, in the new economy profits must come from substantiating value, not from defending price.

Because of the preeminence of customers, controlling the relationship with the customer is much more important than merely controlling the product.[2] Controlling the relationship allows us to support price and this in turn brings us closer to attaining full price. Remember, however, that supporting value is not defending price. It is defining value and making that value so tangible that full price can be demanded.

Discounting, on the other hand, is a dangerous journey on which to embark. It is the proverbial slippery slope. Price cutting cheapens your product or service and dramatically reduces its perceived value. Once your customers believe that the intention of your company is merely to defend price and that discounting is an option, they will most often shift from premium or vacillating customers to transaction customers.

Leading companies realize their focus must always remain on substantiating value. Leaders understand it is not possible in today's ultracompetitive marketplace to serve two masters: price and value.

Smart companies intuitively know that it is impossible to get full price if they are constantly defending high prices. They recognize that their ability to substantiate value will be one of the key determinants in bringing them closer to full price.

Substantiating value is best done in three ways: (1) identifying the process to find full price; (2) identifying those things of tangible value that support full price; and (3) creating a value statement at the organizational level that justifies the value you are seeking to substantiate.

IDENTIFYING THE PROCESS
TO ACHIEVE FULL PRICE

When a company identifies the process unique to its culture that achieves full price, it becomes much easier to substantiate value. Such things as a combination of better product assortment, better service, greater customization, or faster delivery times can all take the focus away from defending price. Each company, however, will have to determine and take this step on its own.

Nortel

Nortel, a telecommunications company that sells telephone systems to small and midsized organizations like law firms, found its customers were constantly looking to cut their price. Like many companies, Nortel realized it could not keep cutting their prices and make a profit. After researching their premium customers' highest needs, Nortel found it could support its prices by promising on-site delivery of its telephone systems within 48 hours.

Although the products Nortel produced were reliable and competitive, the key to supporting price was combining its telephone systems with services people were willing to pay for.[3]

Arbor National Mortgage

In the mortgage industry, the product being sold is money. Seemingly, what else could matter in this category other than price? It should come as no surprise, therefore, that the mortgage business is chronically in a state of discounts and reduced profits. However, even within this apparently hopeless environment, some lenders have actually been able to support their price.

Arbor National Mortgage, a midsize lender in Uniondale, New York, has been able to swim upstream against the tide of cuts and maintain the integrity of its prices. "We never sell products based on price. We focus on niche products, repackaging plain-vanilla mortgages, and relationships with the community," says Nancy Boles, Arbor's senior vice president of marketing.

For example, Arbor takes a standard mortgage and repackages it into the Arbor Home Bridal Registry. Couples register with Arbor instead of a department store so friends and family members can contribute to the newlywed's first home. Arbor also holds mortgage seminars for real estate brokers, accountants, and homebuyers. And the company plants a tree for each customer, either in the customer's yard or a public park.

Such activities have allowed Arbor's revenues to nearly double every year since 1991. Gareth Plank, a mortgage banking analyst with Mabon Securities, may sum it up best when he says, "Arbor simply excels at staying above the fray."[4]

IDENTIFYING ELEMENTS OF TANGIBLE VALUE THAT SUPPORT FULL PRICE

The one thing that sets your product or service apart from the rest is most likely made up of one or more identifiable elements. These clearly defined elements are the tangible things leading companies use to further substantiate value. Again, like identifying the process to find full price, these tangible things are unique to your company and the products and services you sell. By identifying these things, it is much easier to substantiate the value of those products and services and therefore move closer to the full-price ideal.

Okuma America Corporation

Okuma America of Charlotte, North Carolina, manufactures metal-cutting machine tools, including lathes, machine centers, and grinders—machines that other manufacturers rely on for their own production. If Okuma's machines go down, its customers' plants could go down. About four and one-half years ago, the company realized the tangible elements that helped it attain full price were not the quality of its products but the firm's dedication in responding to customer inquiries and the availability of spare parts for its machines.

As a result, Okuma soon realized that distributors and customers on the West Coast, because of the three-hour time difference, were not receiving the same level of service as their East Coast counterparts. To change this, the company added a second shift so that parts and service would be available to all customers across the United States.

The program was so successful that soon the company began offering 24-hour service to all customers, every day of the week, including holidays. This required distributors and key plant personnel to wear beepers, and it involved special negotiations with shipping firms. The customer response was so positive that Okuma then began to promise on-time shipping. If a part arrives late, it's free.

You would think that 24-hour, 7-day service with on-time overnight shipping guarantees would be enough to keep customers happy. But it's not. As Larry Schwartz, senior vice president, explains, "Our customers need parts for their machines immediately— tomorrow isn't good enough anymore." Because of this, the company recently introduced a new line of computerized cutting machines that have the capability of notifying operators, distributors, and the plant people at Okuma when the machines are not "feeling well." If a part is wearing out, the machine itself can call an Okuna distributor via modem. This allows Okuma to send a service rep with the appropriate parts almost before the customer knows there is a problem.

But there's more to the tangible things Okuma has identified to substantiate the value of its products. As efficient as these new machines are, they still require service reps to make calls, and calls take time, no matter how early in the process the reps are notified.

To eliminate the time required for external service altogether, Okuma is experimenting with a type of spare part vending machine in which the most commonly replaced parts will actually be placed at a customer's plant location.

Okuma's substantiation of value through the identification of those tangible things the company does is a response to the demands of its customers. "People don't even want to stand in line at McDonald's," Schwartz says.[5] Price is not an issue for Okuma's customers. Value is.

payANYbill.com

payANYbill.com is a leading online provider that enables small to medium-sized billers to provide their customers with a complete electronic service for bill presentment, bill payment processing, and bill consolidation over the Internet. The Toronto-based company partners with businesses, banks, service bureaus, consolidators, and portals to provide consumers with the ability to pay any bill anytime using any Internet-connected device. payANYbill.com has been able to substantiate its value because of the tangible improvements in efficiency and cost savings over existing paper-intensive bill payment processes.

CREATING A VALUE STATEMENT

The terms *list price, suggested retail price,* or *regular price* are as relevant today as pull-top soda cans and eight-track cassettes. They are dinosaurs of a past age when a company would figure out its fair profit and then try to sell as many or as much as they could for a fair price. Today, however, customers do not want to hear anything about fair price. They incessantly want the best deal.

To overcome this dramatic shift in customer behavior and still be able to substantiate value, smart companies create a value statement that permeates their entire organization. This statement substantiates value rather than defending price.

Saturn

Saturn, for instance, was heralded as a revolutionary within the automobile industry when it introduced itself as a no wheeling or dealing kind of car company. The listed price on the car was defended because Saturn dealers were reported to have far fewer costs than a regular General Motors dealership. For example, Saturn salespeople were paid a salary rather than a commission. Therefore, the customer believed the cost savings to the dealer were being passed on to them. The end result has been a growing customer base for Saturn that gladly pays the list price of each new model—unheard of in the car industry! Saturn's value statement to both the marketplace and its organization is "A New Kind of Car Company."

IDG Books

IDG Books Worldwide, Inc., is one of the leaders in life-long learning products. Its brands range from Cliff Notes to Frommer's to Webster's New World. One of its newest brands, which is also one of its most successful, is the For Dummies series. For Dummies has become one of the leading book series in the world—known for its anxiety-eliminating approach to teaching a wide range of topics, from computers and cooking to personal finance and foreign languages, in a simple and fun manner.

The value statement—For Dummies—dominates the entire organization. All of IDG's books—regardless of the topic—are written in a format that's entertaining, engaging, easy to read, and yet highly detailed. In the marketplace, For Dummies has come to symbolize this format as well. As a result, the books substantiate their value as a useful resource rather than merely defending their price.

Mercedes-Benz USA

To offer customers more than just car sales and service, Mercedes-Benz USA, Inc., (MBUSA) announced that in conjunction with the introduction of the model year 2000 Mercedes-Benz product line, the company and its 312 retail partners would introduce a comprehensive retail-level initiative—called "The Mercedes Experience"—that seeks to create a new benchmark for substantiating value in the automotive industry.

Said Mike Jackson, president and CEO of MBUSA:

> This is a fundamental change in the way the automotive business is conducted at the retail level. We believe the key to success in the new millennium will be to build enduring relationships—relationships on the clients' terms. From the time that someone considers buying a vehicle to the actual purchase or repurchase—and the time in between—each interaction will be a moment of truth. The Mercedes Experience promises our clients not only exciting and innovative products but also enjoyable and convenient business processes; professional, caring people; exceptional value and focused, personal communication.[6]

The creation of the value statement The Mercedes Experience is predicated on the notion that value needs to be dependent on a company's best products and best services. When a company makes value dependent on how and when a client purchases, they attract opportunists, people who are more interested in the deal of the month rather than in the product.

Baskin-Robbins

Baskin-Robbins is traditionally one of the highest-priced ice cream stores around. Yet profits for their stores always seem to be some of the highest in the industry. Why? One reason is because Baskin-Robbins has created a value statement that substantiates the value of its products. "31 Flavors" is a verbal reflection of the process to find full price and the tangible things that substantiate the value of its products. Nobody ever argues with the price of a double-scoop waffle cone at Baskin-Robbins. The value of selecting from 31 different flavors more than offsets any concern customers have about price. And by constantly reminding both its employees and its customers about the selection, 31 Flavors has become part of our lexicon as well as a strong example of a value statement that substantiates value instead of defending price.

SUMMARY

Time and time again we hear about the difficulty companies have in raising their prices much beyond the annual inflation rate, even as their level of service and quality improve. In addition, many companies find that their innovations are quickly replicated by their competitors and often improved. This "commoditization" of products and services tends to keep prices stagnant. As a result, profits need to originate from somewhere else. Increasingly, in the new economy profits must come from substantiating value, not from defending price.

Substantiating value is best done in three ways:

- Identifying the process to find full price

- Identifying those things of tangible value that support full price

- Creating a value statement at the organizational level that justifies the value you are seeking to substantiate

CHAPTER 11

Living
the Brand

*"A great brand promotes high
value that reaches full price."*

—Thom Winninger

Based on the evidence, a brand must be one of the biggest
guns in the arsenal of a company and therefore worthy of significant investment. After all, consumer product companies regularly
spend hundreds of millions to support their brands. Wall Street values leading Internet companies at huge multiples because of their
online brand strength. And CEOs in survey after survey say their
ability to create and maintain strong brands is one of the most important keys to their company's future success.

Without question, brands do in fact make up a large part of
the value of many successful companies. Brands do matter. Across
a wide range of industries, companies that are adept at developing
and managing brands seemingly always reap the rewards. To the
traditional packaged goods giants such as Procter & Gamble have
been added a new breed of successful "branders," from Benetton

to British Airways, from Priceline.com to Disney, and from Versace to Nike. These companies and dozens like them have been extraordinarily successful at using their brands to strengthen their core business and create a platform for expansion.

Still, even while brands can clearly be seen as a pathway to success, many decision makers constantly seem to wrestle with branding issues. Accustomed to talking about profit and expected returns on investment, they suddenly have to make major decisions without a clear understanding of the effects of brands on their earning streams. The results can be problematic: not investing properly in brand development and a misjudgment in setting priorities.

For decades, insurance companies have been among the largest of national advertisers trying to build their brands. They have invested literally billions of dollars promoting devices like umbrellas, horses, cupped hands, towers, signatures, and slogans. If you want a "good neighbor" you turn to State Farm. Prefer to be in "good hands"? Look to Allstate. Need a "rock"? Then call Prudential.

All these companies invested all those advertising dollars building brand by stressing reliability, confidence, longevity, and financial strength. The notion was that the consuming public would seek the agents representing the companies behind the icons to purchase products. And it worked, right?

Not exactly. After investing all those billions, according to Harte-Hanks Market Research, just 16 percent of survey respondents rated the auto insurance industry "excellent." And only 11 percent of respondents rated the insurance segment "excellent." In other words, 84 percent of customers did not think so much of their auto underwriter and 89 percent didn't think a lot of their life insurance company. The lesson: Unless a company truly lives its brand in all facets of its business, the resources spent on building a brand would probably be better thrown to the wind.

Leading companies realize that the proper dedication of their resources toward their brands is fundamental to their long-term growth. First, leaders live their brands both inwardly and outwardly. Second, leaders are aware that living the brand is a combination of long-term focus and short-term actions. And third, leaders grasp that their brands cannot be everything to everybody.

LIVE YOUR BRAND INWARDLY
AND OUTWARDLY

Leaders innately understand that everything they do affects their brand. Stakeholders are those individuals, organizations, or markets that have a strong interest in seeing your company succeed and prosper. Beyond your existing and potential customers, stakeholders may include your company's employees, shareholders, strategic suppliers, the community where your physical operations are located, and your customers' customers. All of these people and groups come together under the umbrella of your company and the brands they represent. Leaders recognize this and devote themselves to communicating what they and their brands are about to their stakeholders. Leaders understand the critical importance of having the most important entities of their organization "all on the same page" and "singing the same song." More important, leaders discern that, if properly informed and communicated with, these stakeholders will become an army of ambassadors for the company's products and services. They will exhort others to examine your brands.

It never ceases to amaze me how many companies I come across that fail to adequately communicate to their employees what the company and its brands are truly all about. There is hardly anybody else who better knows the strengths and weaknesses of your company's products and services than the people who daily participate in the construction and delivery of those same products and services. Yet far too many companies fail to communicate their brand strategies to these most crucial of stakeholders. In these cases, senior management seems to distrust or discount the vital role employees can play in helping a company build its brands and achieve full price.

Leaders proactively take it upon themselves to integrate their employees into the creation and maintenance of their brands. They foster and encourage their employees to play increasingly more important roles in the strategic development of their brands. In Chapter 14 I discuss at length how companies create an environment in which the creativity and knowledge of their employees is best leveraged to help them attain full price.

The widespread proliferation of shareholders in America in recent years has raised the percentage of U.S. households owning stocks or mutual funds from 22 percent in 1990 to over 50 percent today. As a result, publicly traded companies are finding their shareholders make up a much larger and wider cross section of Americans than ever before. The sheer number of individual investors who may hold shares in your company provides a wonderful opportunity to live your brand to that crucial universe of stakeholders.

Your company's strategic suppliers clearly play a fundamental role in the growth and future of your company. Given the increasingly competitive nature of the new economy, your strategic suppliers are probably as close to your company's processes and systems as many of your premium customers. Who better than these invaluable providers to help you live the brand?

The community where your physical operations are located affords a positive venue of stakeholders in which to live your brand. For generations, Ford, General Motors, and Chrysler most effectively communicated their brands in the same cities where their manufacturing plants were located. Stakeholders in places like Flint, Detroit, Cleveland, and Lordstown were, in many cases, numbered in the hundreds of thousands. Employees and their families; local business owners; community leaders; public institutions; not-for-profits; and innumerable other individuals and organizations saw their future tied in some way to the success of the local manufacturing facility.

In addition, many business-to-business companies are realizing that by communicating to the ultimate buyer, they can help their customers increase sales, build profits, and create lasting loyalty. As a result, an emerging trend among business-to-business companies is to transmit their corporate culture and communicate their brands to their customers' customers.

OneLink Corporation

OneLink Corporation, a company based in Eden Prairie, Minnesota, sells report-generation software to regional telephone companies like US West and Cincinnati Bell, which sell telecom services to businesses and consumers. Using that software, OneLink takes the vast sea of call data their clients collect on their business customers, then aggregates the data, analyzes them, and prepares reports— complete with interactive maps, graphs, and charts. The telecom clients in turn sell those customized reports, under their own brands, to their business customers. Moreover, OneLink communicates with their clients' customers to make sure the reports meet those customers' needs.

With these reports, companies of any size can see each caller's phone number; how often each calls and when; each call's duration; the caller's geographic area; and even how many times a given caller got a busy signal before giving up for good. And because incoming calls can be viewed as a trend by time and region, the reports also provide the kind of information most marketers find of high value by allowing companies to correlate call volume to radio ads or target specific marketing campaigns.

Denise Marts, business manager for Midwest Eye Care PC in Omaha, speaks for literally hundreds of US West customers when she called the Call Report Center. "I told them what I wanted, and in a short time they called back with more questions on what I'd like. They told me I'd get a new version in about three months after my first phone call to them." Three months later she had the new version in hand. The reports gave the 12-physician vision clinic a keenly focused eye on marketing and staffing issues. Says Marts, "We had speculated that we were getting 200 calls a day, but our second call report showed we were getting 700 calls a day."[1] The result: fewer missed calls and better customer service.

KeyCorp

KeyCorp, one of the largest retail financial services companies in the United States, has seen its stock market value jump almost logarithmically in the past few years. One of the most important reasons for this growth is that the company offers a common set of products and services nationwide. Moreover, it positions itself clearly by properly living out its brand, Key: KeyBank, KeyCenters, Key Money Management, Key.com.

LONG-TERM FOCUS AND
SHORT-TERM ACTION

Leaders pay constant attention to their actions of today so that they might best meet their expectations and destination for the future.

Lear Corporation

Lear Corporation of Southfield, Michigan, is a leading designer and manufacturer of almost every component found inside a car, truck, or minivan of practically every automaker in the world. Like most manufacturers, Lear's industry is incredibly competitive. To best respond to those competitive pressures, the world's carmakers have focused on what *they* do best—engine development and exterior design—and mandated that their suppliers take a larger, more responsible role in what they do best. To better live its brand, Lear has taken it upon itself to regularly recruit hundreds of car buyers to look, feel, and sit in practically every vehicle in practically every category. The company's technicians also tear apart every vehicle Lear has leased to measure, photograph, and quantify every combination of factors that make a great car seat, a comfortable armrest, or an ergonomic cockpit. And it works. "Lear is an example of a company that has gone above and beyond getting in touch with the customer," says Ben Lever, executive vice president at Ford Motor Company. "They are definitely worth more to us, and definitely a preferred supplier because they have communicated their strong research effort to us." Such a dedication to communicating with clients and stakeholders allows Lear to better live its brand.[2]

Target

Not so long ago, if you thought of Target at all, you probably just regarded it as one of the indistinguishable mass merchants in a country seemingly already overflowing with retail stores. Still,

Target has almost by stealth become the nation's third largest retailer. Celebrities are now being photographed in Target gear and using Target labeled products. The designer Michael Graves is exclusively offering his latest work at Target, where his cutting-edge and unbelievably popular fashions have caused near riots from Princeton to Cleveland to Omaha.

In a word, Target is hot. Going to Target has become a cool experience and everybody now considers it cool to save money. On the other hand, is it cool to save at Kmart and Wal-Mart? Not nearly as much. Rival marts have achieved growth with expanded stores, inventory prowess, and rock-bottom prices. All fundamentally sound ideas, but they provide little in the way of brand differentiation. After all, any retailer can lure shoppers with deep discounts. Target's strategy, on the other hand, has been much subtler: Stick to low prices, of course, but rise above the rest with an upmarket brand and design. In other words, price like a discounter but don't live the brand like one.

To see Target's unique positioning in action, just grab one of the store's red plastic carts and work your way through its signature white, shiny linoleum aisles. There are no dim fluorescent lights, no Wal-Mart type stacks of corn flakes everywhere. Target's merchandising brilliance owes much to its department store heritage. Visual clutter is forbidden on the 133,000-square-foot floor. A third of the space is devoted to apparel, the rest to hard lines such as housewares and electronics. Low-margin dog food is displayed next to high-margin ceramic dog bowls. A lip gloss named Fetish mimics the chic Stila brand in both packaging and color except that it costs $4 a tube instead of $16.

Target is always seeking the latest products, whether cameras or skirts. So if the home decor section at Wal-Mart seems dated— a candlestick here, a lampshade there—Target's Restore and Restyle section features chic brass door pulls, and hotel-style towel racks. If Kmart gives dinnerware 16 feet of display space, Target will do it with 32, ample room for its enamel imports. This sort of lifestyle merchandising helps Target do more than nibble the market share of the Kmarts or even the J.C. Penneys of the world.

Target lives the brand in other ways as well. In 1995, Target became the first mart to offer a proprietary credit card. Over 12 million cards have been issued to date, making it the fastest card rollout in retail history. Next, Target launched Club Wedd, its version of a bridal registry. Just three years old, Club Wedd is now among the nation's largest bridal registries along with Macy's and J.C. Penney.

The payoff is that Target's "expect more pay less" brand statement is resounding with a more affluent demographic than any other store in its class. The chain's average customer is female and college educated, with a household income near $50,000. At 40, she's younger than most mart shoppers. All this helps to explain the average store check at Target is $40—almost twice as much as that of other mass merchants. It seems that as people used to say, "Ooh, a Nordstrom's is coming to town," those same people now say, "Ooh, we're getting a Target!"[3]

BRANDS CANNOT BE EVERYTHING TO EVERYBODY

In too many cases, companies have outbranded themselves; that is, they have allowed their brands to become so extensive and diverse that their original purpose and intent becomes too diluted. General Motors is probably no longer a brand. It has no intrinsic meaning. The General Motors brand has become totally diluted, overshadowed by Pontiac, Chevrolet, and Saturn. Disney, although still a viable brand in its own right, is in danger of losing its advantage through its identification with subsidiaries like ABC, ESPN, and TouchTone Pictures. Such a proliferation can be dangerous if one of the related brands experiences difficulty in the marketplace.

Also, the nature and economics of a product will often determine how hard a customer will work to obtain information about it. And that, in turn, determines in many cases the dynamics of the brand. Such dynamics may include not only the value of brand in a given market but whether a single brand will be sufficient to support multiple market niches.

3M–Minnesota Mining and Manufacturing

3M's branding decisions for its lines of clear adhesive tapes are based on how much attention consumers pay adhesive tape. According to 3M, the Scotch and Highland brands are kept separate because they offer distinctly different levels of quality. Scotch, the premium brand, can be removed from paper without tearing the paper's surface. Lower-priced Highland will tear the paper and appears less transparent. Because 3M knows that few customers will take the time to read the specifications of its adhesive tape, the only way to clearly signal the distinction in quality is to brand the two tapes separately. Each has a different market focus: Scotch appeals to the price insensitive, whereas Highland competes with discount brands of adhesive tape.

BMW

In contrast to 3M, car manufacturers have the luxury of knowing that most of their customers view a car as a major purchase and will invest time in investigating their options. Thus, car manufacturers can support multiple levels of quality under the single umbrella of the company brand. BMW wants potential purchasers to believe that it produces the "Ultimate Driving Machine" at different price levels. Although its low-end 3-Series may very well underperform some other cars, BMW knows consumers will have the sophistication to understand that, for its class, the 3-Series nonetheless offers superior handling. BMW realizes that at the end of the day, companies don't own brands, customers do. By treating its customers accordingly, the BMW marquee remains the only branding required.

PricewaterhouseCoopers

In the high-stakes consulting marketplace, customers are seeking help from companies with proven expertise. Having a brand identity that emphasizes a company's knowledge can pay big dividends. PricewaterhouseCoopers (PWC), a consulting company based in New York, has found a high-tech way to live its brand as an expert in the telecommunications arena. The company teamed up with the PointCast Network, a free service that offers up-to-the-minute information on such topics as entertainment, finance, and world affairs via a number of online channels. It also signed on with PointCast to run the Telecom Insider—a three-channel block devoted to telecommunications.

As a way to ensure the branding initiative would be worth the money, PWC hired focus groups and passed out surveys to its best customers—senior executives. Not surprisingly, research showed that busy executives were seeking convenient information and high content that would help them make sound business decisions. Now, to get breaking information to executives, Telecom Insider is patched into cell phones, Palm Pilots, and pagers so users can have instant access to Telecom Insider's information. PWC also produces a separate Web site that features a searchable archive of the articles on the Insider. PWC's investment with PointCast and the creation of Telecom Insider helps PWC live its brand as a thought leader in the telecommunications industry.

Sony

Sony Corporation of America has been successfully developing an umbrella brand strategy that ties in all of its electronic and content assets, making Sony the number one digital entertainment company in the world. The foundation of the company rests on electronic devices. Since the Walkman appeared in 1980, Sony has been synonymous with leading-edge consumer electronics: TV sets, HDTV sets, portable radios, and tape and CD players evolving to include set-top boxes, personal computers, and devices to download and play Internet music. Sony also owns PlayStation, the gaming platform; The Station, an online gaming platform; and reams of content, starting with a major Hollywood studio, thousands of hours of current and old TV shows as well as a wide range of artists from Tony Bennett to Bruce Springsteen to the Dixie Chicks.

To harness such a broad array of products and live one fluid brand, Sony has begun to create synergies between its different divisions. For instance, Ford held a contest to send some lucky *Dawson's Creek* fan—a Sony-owned TV program—to the set of the hit TV show in Wilmington, North Carolina. Sony record artists then played at a special concert held in Wilmington the next day.

Sony's releases of *Charlie's Angels* and *Spiderman* both have tags added to the current and future Sony consumer electronic devices, such as phones and portable music players. Such strategic thinking across seemingly disparate product lines allows Sony to leverage all of its assets seamlessly and therefore live its singular brand to all of its premium customers.

SUMMARY

Leading companies realize that the proper dedication of their resources toward their brands is fundamental to their long-term growth. Leaders do the following:

- Live their brands both inwardly and outwardly

- Recognize that living the brand is a combination of long-term focus and short-term actions

- Grasp that their brands cannot be everything to everybody

147

CHAPTER 12

Exploiting Technology

> *"Smart companies instinctively understand the Internet is a means to an end, not the end itself."*
>
> —Thom Winninger

Every Saturday afternoon in December 1999, San Francisco's Union Square, the city's premiere shopping district, was totally out of control. Thousands of shoppers laden with bags pushed each other along the pavement, desperately searching for one of the few empty taxis or struggling to get through Macy's doors to buy the one last gift for that somebody special. But wait: Surely Christmas shopping in 1999 was to be different, especially so close to Silicon Valley, the heart of the Internet revolution and the new economy. New billionaires and their dot.com employees were supposed to have bought all of their presents on the Web the day after Thanksgiving. Yet the crowds in Union Square were worse than ever.

The shoppers seemed totally oblivious to the large billboard announcement above their heads for one of the Bay Area's many Internet retailers that read, "Say Goodbye to the Mall." And the shoppers seemingly paid no attention to the advertisement on many of their shopping bags that pointed a way out of the chaos: "Online Shopping. No Experience Needed."

Electronic commerce, it seems, still has its limits, even in Silicon Valley. Does that mean, however, that its much-hyped arrival is more sky than substance—rather as it is for the share values of most of the dot.coms themselves? For all of the feverish media exposure and anticipation of electronic shopping in the 1999 holiday season, the total purchased by American consumers online still amounted to about 1 percent of all retail sales—barely one-tenth of the revenues from another method of distance selling that has been around for more than a century: the catalog. Moreover, electronic shopping was concentrated on a very narrow range of goods—mainly books, toys, and music. Also, more and more hacker attacks temporarily disable some of the best known e-commerce Web sites. Perhaps retailers in the physical world need not lose much sleep over the Internet, or at least not yet.

Yet they are losing sleep and are right to be doing so. It is undeniable that the powerful potential of the development and application of new technology will allow companies to do new things and, indeed, do many old things better. And despite the teething troubles, business-to-consumer electronic commerce will grow significantly, and that will be especially important for certain kinds of goods and services. It is therefore bound to have a huge impact on offline commerce as well. Goldman Sachs estimates that the rise of e-commerce will cause average growth in offline retail sales to slow down from 5 to 3 percent.

But even with all of this, it is critical for traditional businesses to look at the rise of the Internet and the growth of e-commerce from a realistic perspective. That is, to not allow themselves to be consumed by the incessant hype that is dominating the press and the business world about how the Internet will change everything. One of the saddest stories of a product that was driven by the hype and failed to take a step back and look at the information technology and the Internet in an objective way is one of the oldest and finest consumer products ever sold.

The notion of an encyclopedia was essentially a product of the Enlightenment. In France, Dennis Diderot devoted a lifetime to producing one. But what was to become the most famous encyclopedia in the world started in 1768 in Edinburgh, Scotland: Encyclopaedia Britannica. As it went through successive editions, academics and ordinary readers alike came to rely on it.

The reputation of Encyclopaedia Britannica survived a change in ownership when Sears Roebuck, an upstart catalog company, bought it and moved it to the New World city of Chicago. Two decades later it became the property of a foundation, the proceeds of which benefited the University of Chicago. Its door-to-door salesmen became legendary for their knack of persuading parents that an encyclopedia was a must if their children were to become well-educated adults. By 1989, sales revenues had reached a record $650 million, and the firm's salesforce had grown to 2,300.

Yet disaster was waiting in the wings. It began when Microsoft produced a cheap CD-ROM called Encarta in 1993. Britannica's directors responded with a CD of their own, but their salespeople rebelled at seeing their hardcover books undercut. The Internet made things infinitely worse. Britannica sales collapsed along with its salesforce. In 1995 the company changed hands again for a small fraction of its book value. Today it employs fewer than 350 people. In October 1999, the new owner decided to make the contents of the Encyclopaedia Britannica available for free on the Internet in the optimistic hope of recouping the cost through advertising on its Web site. But as if to question even this new strategy, the site promptly crashed.

What lesson should be drawn from this? If you are engaged in almost any form of commerce, from the humble mom-and-pop enterprise to the gigantic department store, the information technology and the Internet are lurking like an invisible opponent, ready to dramatically impact your business. Still, for all of its bluster, the eventual elimination of bricks and mortar at the hands of electronic commerce simply isn't going to happen. Certainly, e-commerce will force many business processes and activities to adapt or fall by the wayside. However, like the catalog, e-commerce will evolve and eventually find its place alongside the traditional methods of selling products and services to consumers.

To succeed with information technology and the Internet, companies have to know what they've always needed to know: what their best customers really want. Whether it is a Web site or a retail brick-and-mortar establishment, critical attention to customer needs has to drive a company's strategic planning.

Peter Drucker, the legendary father of modern management, probably said it best when he was asked in a recent interview what he thought about the future of information technology and the Internet: "I am not unimpressed with the potential of technology. But I am very surprised that computer people pay no attention at all to where they have made the greatest impact. Yesterday, I saw a tone-deaf piano tuner use a computer to tune a piano. He did exactly what piano tuners have done for 300 years, but the software did it. The same is true for tax returns, payroll, and architectural drawings: The greatest impact is that traditional operations have been automated. A grand piano tuning used to take 3 hours; this one took 11 minutes."

Drucker went on to say, "I think there's going to be no shortage of people who are computer literate. In this country, a very large percentage of the children are not only computer literate but information-technology literate. Unlike the current generations, my grandchildren not only know how to use a computer, they understand what it can do!" In other words, information technology simply for the sake of information technology is not enough.

Leading companies are the ones that will not be exploited by technology but instead will exploit it as another tool to meet and exceed the highest needs of their best customers. Leaders recognize that they need to execute combined online and offline strategies that reinforce already existing merchandising strengths and enhance the inherent power of their brands. They clearly see that effective marketing, not technology, is the key driver of Internet and e-commerce success. Technology might be the platform, but it commoditizes quickly and therefore loses its value.

Leaders view the proper exploitation of technology in three ways. First, they see the Internet and information technology as a preselling opportunity to communicate their traditional customer values and reach out to a wider audience. Second, leaders view the Internet as an effective way in which to inform their customers as well as the marketplace at large about their products and services. Third, leaders use the Internet to conduct transactions that complement rather than cannibalize or even harm their brands.

THE INTERNET AND TECHNOLOGY AS INFORMATION VEHICLES

The power available to the consumer through access to the Internet is unprecedented. For much less than a dollar a day, consumers can search millions of available Web sites for the information they want in less time than it takes to find one phone number in the Yellow Pages. Further, the Web's reach is global, so it ought to be able to outdo the physical world in many aspects of information gathering.

In a recent survey by Cyveillance, Inc., it was found that, surprisingly, less than one-fifth of Web sites offering travel, brokerage, and electronic equipment are able to handle sales transactions. According to Cyveillance, there are some 116,000 travel sites, 7,400 online brokerages, and 6,600 sites that feature electronics and gadgets. Only about 6,500 of those travel sites, 2,000 of the trading sites, and 400 of the electronics sites actually let customers execute transactions online. This then begs the important question: What are these tens of thousands of nontransacting sites really doing if they're not selling anything? The answer: providing information. Leading companies realize that the Internet and information technology provide them with a tremendous opportunity to transmit real-time news and information to their customers and the marketplace at large.

Blockbuster

Blockbuster Video, the leading videotape rental firm in the world, also possesses the largest customer list in the industry. To better inform all those customers about their products, Blockbuster has been methodically updating its Web site, constantly adding more entertainment content. Blockbuster is using its Web presence to drive its existing customers and, more important, new ones to its stores through the transmission of information relevant to those same customers. Users of Blockbuster's Web site can click on video trailers for new releases and receive periodic e-mail product announcements.

Enhancing relationships with dealer and distribution channels can also be accomplished by using information technology and the Internet.

Compaq Computer

Houston-based Compaq Computer Corporation has created strong partnerships with its resellers and retailers by using the Internet to promote its products. Before the advent of the Internet, Compaq had to put together product kits for its resellers and send them by mail. They had to constantly send out kits and many times found the reseller never even bothered to open the promotional products. Now that the Internet has become the primary means of communication between Compaq and its customers, there is no longer a problem with resellers getting outdated and useless information. With the click of a mouse, they can browse Compaq's Web site for their individual needs. Product updates are not the only things dealers can get from the Web. The Internet can benefit a dealer's or distributor's incentive program by allowing quick access to information. Dealers who participate in incentive programs can use the Internet to check their quotas, accumulated points, and award categories.

Compaq, like countless other companies, has found that distributors and internal salesforces are expecting accelerated delivery of service and a seamless resolution of challenges. The old way of doing business required a lot of paper. As a result of that tedious process, there was invariably a lag time in fulfillment. Now, with enhanced access to timely information, Compaq's distributors and salesforces receive up-to-date service.

Compaq has been successful in leveraging the experience of information technology at the retail level as well. To accommodate consumers who prefer to go to the local brick-and-mortar computer vendor to touch the merchandise, Compaq introduced its Built for You Kiosk in 9,600 retail stores nationwide. The kiosk enables consumers to go to a store and configure the product they want on-site. If they have questions, the store's staffers are still there to assist them.

As customer service on the Web evolves, companies continue adding features to their service. The most common option for on-line customer information is text chat. Companies that offer this service add a box to their Web site that allows customers to contact an agency by clicking a button. Customers enjoy the opportunity to help themselves.

Cintas

Cintas Corporation, a Mason, Ohio–based uniform manufacturer, was one of the first in its industry to use chat-based software. It allows a customer service representative (CSR) to be more efficient by using preformatted responses that allow the CSRs to answer customer questions more quickly, efficiently, and effectively. Cintas's agents can handle up to four chats at once. And, according to the company, customers who participate in a chat are more likely to buy. The average online conversion rate for the industry is between 1 and 5 percent. However, customers who participate in a live chat with a CSR buy 25 to 30 percent of the time.

THE INTERNET AND TECHNOLOGY AS COMMUNICATION VEHICLES

Window shopping on the Web has become one of a consumer's favorite activities. Leaders recognize that one of the applications of their e-commerce strategy, like the mail-order catalog, is to better inform the marketplace about their brick-and-mortar facilities. However, in the age of the Internet, providing customer value means much more than just being able to answer basic product-oriented or service-oriented questions.

Leading companies have a Web presence that makes it easy for customers to inquire about merchandise, check the status of their orders, file complaints, or send compliments—all without having to pick up the phone. Companies effectively communicate the necessary information their customers need to make the relationship a stronger one. Leaders conceptualize that their ability to communicate to their customers via the Web is a larger part of the sales process. Instead of seeing each request or inquiry as a single interaction, smart companies view Internet communication as a critical element of the entire customer experience through which they can glean valuable information to keep the customer coming back.

Southwest Airlines

One company that has found great success with the Internet as a communicator of its brands is the Dallas-based carrier Southwest Airlines. Since the launch of its Web site in 1995, it has received an enormous volume of hits from its customer base year after year. Southwest has consciously striven to provide the same service online as they do offline. As an added perk for online users, Southwest constantly sponsors sweepstakes for vacations and also offers a customer loyalty program, known as Rapid Rewards, which awards frequent flyers various perks. Members can log on to a customer service representative and access their accounts directly from the Web site.

Exploiting technology doesn't mean a company has to compromise quality in the process. Although Southwest provides its customers with complementary channels to book flights and get schedules, it still has maintained the objective of providing high-quality customer service. Staying away from automated solutions, which are readily made available by some other Web sites, Southwest Airlines puts the power in the customer's hands. At the Web site, customers can search for the information they need and take their time. In the past, Rapid Rewards statements would be sent to customers and it was practically out of date by the time customers had it in their hands. Customers who are really involved with the Rapid Rewards accounts can look it up every day if they want to. That kind of communication was not possible without the Web site.

Budget Rent a Car

Budget Rent a Car Corporation gives customers the opportunity to participate in the Simple Drive program through the use of traditional promotional collateral on the Internet. The Simple Drive program offers Budget Rent a Car customers the opportunity to earn points as they rent cars. The points can be redeemed for such products as golf clubs or ski equipment. The loyalty Web site allows Budget's customers to look at their point balances and redeem points online. More important, the Web site provides the consumer the ability to click on the selection of vehicles and actually see them on the road. In such a manner, Budget is providing its tech-savvy customers the ability to communicate with them in the form they prefer.

THE INTERNET AND TECHNOLOGY AS COMPLEMENTARY

Leading companies exploit information technology and the Internet as "complementors" to their products and services. They are able to fight off the short-term impulse to cannibalize their brands and instead use the Internet to enhance the products and services they offer the marketplace.

Longs Drugs Stores

Longs Drugs Stores, a northern California–based chain, has used the Internet to build greater support for its brick-and-mortar stores. Its Web site uses technology to complement the information and communication already provided to Longs' customers. A personalized and customized page allows customers to reorder their prescriptions online and receive them by mail. If customers want to pick up prescriptions in person, they'll be sent an e-mail informing them when the order is ready and thus avoiding long waiting lines, especially over weekends and in the evening.

U.S. Office Products

U.S. Office Products (USOP) Company, a $2.6 billion office products supplier, was playing catch-up with the competition when it finally launched its e-commerce strategy in 1997. Unclear about what the ultimate goal was, U.S. Office Products initiated its Web site to complement existing business by offering customers another way to place orders beyond telephone and fax. Within a few months, the application paid for itself, but a more profound benefit was unforeseen: Business customers that place orders on the Web order less often, but their orders are more than twice as large as when they send them by fax or phone. The reason is that online customers tend to keep an order building all day long.

Although the payback was quick, it is the unanticipated benefits that promise to be most significant. Every time a U.S. Office Products business customer places an order, USOP employees pull products from warehouse shelves, pack them up, and ship the order out. Preparing one large order is more efficient than preparing several smaller ones. When customers primarily ordered by phone, USOP's average order size was $50. Now it is $140.

The Internet has allowed companies to effectively focus on their strengths and rely on other companies to outsource and integrate products and services in which they may not be proficient. Every industry has so many players that there is a strong potential for partnerships, alliances, mergers, and consolidations. Leading companies often increase their market share and complement their brands through partnerships rather than inventing everything from scratch.

SUMMARY

Leading companies are the ones that will not be exploited by technology but instead will exploit it as another tool to meet and exceed the highest needs of their best customers. Leaders recognize that they need to execute combined online and offline strategies that reinforce already existing merchandising strengths and enhance the inherent power of their brands. This is best accomplished by using the Internet and information technology in three ways:

- As a communication tool

- As a provider of information

- As a complement to companys' existing brands

CHAPTER 13

Forging the Indestructible System

"It is not the idea but the system that supports market position over time."

—Thom Winninger

Simply put, leaders turn their ideas into indestructible systems. Two of the best examples are probably Ray Kroc at McDonald's and Henry Ford. Both men were visionaries of their day, inspired by wonderful ideas that changed the world. Their success is obviously due to many factors—one of the more important being the forging of a functional system around their new idea.

Leader companies turn their ideas into a system. Then they make the system functional. Finally, they build their organization around the key attributes of that system.

TURN YOUR IDEA INTO A SYSTEM

For McDonald's, hamburgers and french fries in a quick period of time was the idea, fast food was the system. For Ford Motor Company, the idea was a car for the average American; the assembly line was the system. These and other companies were able to take their notion of what might work and root it in a process-driven foundation.

Recent years have seen the explosion of outlet malls across the country. The system that provides "the ultimate shopping experience" is becoming one of the most popular activities in the country. In Virginia, the home of George Washington's Mount Vernon and Thomas Jefferson's Monticello, the number one attraction is an outlet mall, Potomac Mills, which draws 25 million shoppers and is not the only mall topping a list of the most popular destinations. Near Fort Lauderdale, Sawgrass Mills, the world's largest outlet mall with more than 270 shops, falls second only to Disney World. And the new Opry Mills, located near Nashville's Grand Ole Opry, is already outdrawing Tennessee's top attraction, the Great Smoky Mountains.

Further, the Travel Industry Association of America confirms that outlet shopping malls have become destinations unto themselves. Some 37 percent of all American travelers visited an outlet mall during 1999, and one in ten cite the outlet mall experience as the main reason for their trip. Certainly, the newest outlet malls are reaching theme park proportions, embracing what the Mills Corporation calls "shoppertainment." Besides dashing from Ann Taylor's Loft to Barney's New York, mallgoers are given the option of a virtual reality video game at GameWorks, a twirl on an indoor ice rink, or angling for trout in Bass Pro Shops' indoor pond.

Les Otten

Ski resorts, like snowmobile and snowblower dealers, are too often at the whim of the weather. A lot of snow over a given winter more than makes up for the traditionally slow spring and summer months. On the other hand, not enough snow in the winter can set a business back several years. Probably more than any other individual, Les Otten is credited with helping make the eastern ski resorts less dependent on the fancy of Mother Nature than anyone else. It was Les Otten who forged the indestructible system of making snow.

In the 1970s, Otten, a distinguished student at Ithaca College in upstate New York, took a job as assistant general manager at the Sunday River Ski Resort in Maine. In those days, Sunday River was a sleepy area that attracted—in a high snowfall year—around 40,000 skiers a year. By 1980 Otten was general manager, and when the owners decided to sell, Otten borrowed $840,000 and bought the area himself. Blessed with an ample water supply, Sunday River's expansion proceeded on the reliability of its man-made snow. In fact, to get the message across, one winter he trucked snow and placed it on Boston Common. Today, Sunday River is now the largest ski resort in Maine with 526,000 visitors per year.

MAKE THE SYSTEM FUNCTIONAL

Fast food meant the system of grill to bag to drive-through window or counter. The assembly line meant putting the car together in one place over a short period. Leading companies make their system functional.

Just as self-service pumps have become the norm in most states, self-serve supermarkets are seemingly around the corner. Grocery chains increasingly are introducing self-checkout systems in their express lanes to reduce the time a customer may have to wait. Supermarkets typically leave lanes closed because either they limit how many cashiers they hire or they cannot find enough individuals to fill job openings. And when lanes are closed, customers often must wait in line to pay for groceries.

U-Check

In Salem, Utah, the first fully self-cashiering supermarket called U-Check was recently opened. The parent firm, International Automated Systems, Inc. (IAS), an American Fork, Utah–based company, is beginning to sell the system to franchisees as part of a national rollout. CEO Neldon Johnson, who installed his first self-service cashiering system in 1984, says the system will change the way supermarkets do business. The IAS system, which can accommodate 24 lanes or more, eliminates lines because lanes are always open. Johnson says the system is designed to reduce labor costs by up to 60 percent, reduce so-called shrinkage associated with employee theft and other losses by up to 50 percent, and increase profitability from the traditional 1.5 percent of gross sales to as high as 10 percent.

At the point of sale, consumers wave the items they are buying in front of a bar code scanner, then place them in a cart on a scale. The scanner will not operate if the weight of the cart does not match the weight of the merchandise scanned. "It has to be the correct weight for the scanner to stay on," Johnson says. "If it stays off, a controller has a video to review the last product scanned or the last action that caused the error." In addition, unless the customer is a U-Check debit card holder whose age is already posted in the system, the scanner will lock when someone tries to buy liquor until a supermarket assistant verifies the individual's age and overrides the safety system.

After all the items have been scanned, the customer swipes the debit card through a reader on the terminal and places a finger on a pad to create a separate finger algorithm that is compared against the one on the card. A copy of the finger algorithm is kept on file in the database with the transaction information. A digitized photo of the customer is also kept if the store wants to use that option for reviewing the validity of transactions when disputes arise. A separate cashier station enables customers to pay by check. The cashier also handles any cash and bank debit and credit card transactions, though the self-checkout lanes are being modified to accept those forms of payments.

After customers pay for their merchandise, they walk up to automated exits where they place their carts for a final weight verification. On approval, the gate opens and customers can either bag their own merchandise or receive bagging assistance.

By 2001, IAS expects to have 25 U-Check franchises in place nationally. Concludes Johnson, "This could spark off an entire shift in the retail market because convenience is everything. It's similar to gas stations—when you go half-and-half with self-service you benefit neither the customer nor the business owner. The owner still has to have a person there to pump gas, and the customer still has to wait in line."[1]

As ease of purchase becomes more important in the life of most consumers, many different businesses are forming strategic alliances to provide higher-quality service to their customers. If done properly, the benefits can be truly astounding. One such example of this coming together is the growing number of convenience store operators who, driven by a desire to offer more to their best customers, have migrated into the fast-food business.

The Pantry Store

The Pantry Store in North Belle Vernon, Pennsylvania, has two separate systems, one for the Hardee's fast-food outlet and one for the convenience store, running. According to J.R. Matthews, CEO of The Pantry Store, having separate islands of automation is not a huge problem. "We have good systems for each area," Matthews says. "Still, full integration is something we anticipate being able to do in the future."

Convenience stores that have expanded into the fast-food business find that they need to integrate fast food and convenience store operating systems to avoid installing multiple systems or hiring a number of persons to run them. Clearly, the functions of food service management systems are more intricate than convenience store systems that track whole bags of chips and bottles of Coke as single units.

Minit Mart Foods

Probably the most sophisticated operator in the area of automation is Bowling Green, Kentucky–based Minit Mart Foods, whose 12 superstores operate a minimum of two fast-food outlets in addition to a drive-through, convenience store, and gasoline pumps.

According to Minit Mart's Director of Information Services John Hervery, the management software programs that run each of the areas are seamlessly integrated into a single seamless system. As a result, all registers in all the stores can handle any transaction. Says Hervery, "Even the drive-through can handle video rentals. This allows us to give our customers the best service possible."[2]

BUILD YOUR ORGANIZATION AROUND THE ATTRIBUTES OF THE SYSTEM

McDonald's has people in place that allows it to implement the functions of the system in a fast, efficient way. Ford Motor Company integrated the autoworker into the assembly process. Leaders build their organization around the key functions of their system.

Kinko's

For some, the mention of Kinko's conjures up memories of repressed, overcaffeinated college students and harried execs pulling all-nighters to meet project deadlines. However, over the past few years, Kinko's has become much more than simply a 24-hour place to make copies. It has become a full-service company fully focused on being customer driven. Now, at every Kinko's across the world, you can check your e-mail, scan pictures of grandchildren onto their Web site, design and produce a professional color brochure, bind your latest report, or perform any other number of business-related services.

Kinko's realized that the exponential rise of small businesses in recent years, many of them home based, has led to the need for the outsourcing of basic, but critical, functions. Most small business owners simply do not have the time or resources to focus on tasks that are not directly linked to immediate revenues. As a result, small business owners are increasingly looking for one-stop-shopping solutions for a larger number of tasks that they either cannot or do not want to do. Therefore, my travel agency has become my company's travel department. My lawyer is the legal department. My accountant is the finance department. For millions of businesses all over the world, Kinko's has become their administration, marketing, and information technology departments.

The tremendous success of Kinko's efforts is, in many ways, intricately tied to the seamless system surrounding the wide variety of services offered to its customers. On entering a Kinko's location, customers are guided to the area of their particular need by friendly signs where they easily find instructions and help from an employee trained in that specialty. With a premium placed on attention to unique customer needs, Kinko's goes the extra mile to make sure there are always enough work areas and available staff. Such attention to detail makes Kinko's system a leader in the industry.

The rise of customer call centers in almost every imaginable industry has placed a burden on companies to create an interaction experience that is both efficient and seemingly without flaws.

PNC Bank

Pittsburgh-based PNC Bank has forged a strong call system at its National Financial Services Center. It uses software that requires customers to punch in a PIN or Social Security number. The individual's identity is determined, and that person's past transactions with the bank are immediately analyzed to map the customer into one of several preset needs-based segments.

Callers with rudimentary transactions are transferred to an entry-level representative. Callers with complex financial histories are given to handlers with a specific expertise, most likely tailored to each customer's needs. And a "most valuable customer" is routed to a relationship consultant—one of 30 or 40 service representatives deemed the bank's very best.

Callers have expressed surprise at getting an immediate, effective response from a service representative. It seems banking customers have grown accustomed to punching telephone buttons for several minutes before getting help. But the flexibility of

PNC's interaction system gives service representatives the ability to respond immediately to almost any inquiry.

GTE Internetworking

By integrating Web-based chats into its customer service system, GTE Internetworking is able not only to identify its high-potential customers but also to generate additional sales from them. The idea came from GTE Internetworking's outsourced provider TeleSales, Inc., which designs and implements customized marketing and sales strategies. Using WebLine Communications' Collaboration Server software, TeleSales service reps share information with GTE's customers or help them solve problems via the Web by conducting a voice conversation or text chat. The system is simple: Customers click a callback button that requests a phone call from an agent. The request is routed to a TeleSales agent, who can speak with the customer on the phone while both parties simultaneously browse the Web.

Through the end of 1999, Telesales' agents received more than 5,000 inbound inquiries from prospective GTE Internetworking customers. Phone calls accounted for 57 percent of these leads; e-mail accounted for 35 percent; and 8 percent were from Web customers who clicked on the callback button. The percentage of A-Level leads resulting from the callback button was a staggering 55 percent, in comparison with 35 percent from phone calls and a paltry 4 percent from e-mail. Jeanne Lambert, president and CEO of TeleSales, says that an A-Level lead is a customer who has a need, a budget, and an immediate time frame of 90 days or less for purchasing something. Lambert believes that GTE received more A-Level leads from the Web because customers can instantly contact a customer service representative. This is confirmed by GTE's Internetworking's results, which show that Web-based leads are converted to sales at a rate of 5.5 percent.[3]

SUMMARY

Leaders understand that without a functional system their ideas are worth much less. Leaders forge an indestructible system that builds long-term value that, in turn, supports their market position. Leaders accomplish this by doing the following:

- Turning their ideas into systems

- Then making the system functional

- Finally, building their organization around the key attributes of that system

CHAPTER 14

Building the Right Team

"To make the system work, you have to build the right team."

—Thom Winninger

To develop effective, long-term relationships with their best and most profitable customers, leading companies viscerally realize they must also develop effective, long-term relationships with valuable employees who are able and willing to serve those customers. Ritz-Carlton's credo, "Ladies and gentlemen serving ladies and gentlemen," gets it about right.

Yet I see far too many companies who fail to understand that at the end of the day, their most valuable resource is not their products or services, or even their market or brand strategies, but instead those people who interact and connect with the organization's customers on a regular basis. There is impressive evidence that retaining valued employees is directly connected to value growth.

In its annual look at the 100 best companies to work for, *Fortune* magazine found five-year annual returns of 27.5 percent versus 17.3 percent in the Russell 3000. In a study completed at the beginning of 2000, Ernst & Young found that investors have eight criteria that directly influence their decisions; one is "companies that attract and retain the very best people." Welborne and Andrews, Inc., studied the five-year survival rate of initial public offerings (IPOs) and found companies that cited employees as a key competitive edge were nearly ten times more likely to be around than companies that didn't. In other words, building the right team means a lot to the very existence and survivability of an organization.

Accordingly, given the critical value inherent in building the right team, we would think that companies across North America are actively pursuing this strategy, especially given the volatile employment market that currently exists. myjobsearch.com, one of the premiere jobseeker sites on the Web, recently announced the results of a new survey of worker attitudes about loyalty, which revealed that more than two-thirds of American workers are willing to leave their present employer for a new job that offers as little as a 10 percent improvement in salary. The survey echoes findings by the U.S. Department of Labor that the average 32-year-old has held nine full-time or part-time jobs since entering the workforce. Several factors contributing to the lack of worker loyalty include the lowest national unemployment rate in more than 30 years; turnover at an all-time high, with workers now changing jobs approximately every two and a half years, according to the U.S. Bureau of Labor Statistics; and the fact that companies report spending more each year on recruitment.

However, because of the difficulties faced by employers in this kind of environment, many companies tend to focus on process rather than people. They seem to be saying, "If we're never going to be able to get and hold on to good people, then we might as well dedicate our limited resources to our business processes." Although this may be the most expedient way to deal with the difficulty in finding and keeping good people, it comes up short on addressing the long-term problem.

Leading companies are the ones who have the right culture and procedures in place that enable them to identify, retain, and develop the right employees. Moreover, they are able to place their employees into the proper structure that allows the company to build the right team. Leaders build the right team by tailoring their people to the functions that support the execution of their system; exciting their employees about staying with them for the long term; and recognizing that building a team is an ongoing process.

TAILOR YOUR EMPLOYEES TO YOUR COMPANY'S FUNCTIONS

Smart companies recruit to the functions of the position, not merely to the title of the position. For example, instead of hiring a receptionist, hire someone who possesses the skills and knowledge necessary to function as a receptionist. The key is not the job description but the functions of the position. The same should go for promotions. When moving somebody up from within, leaders are certain the person possesses the critical skills necessary to successfully function in the position. Leaders' emphasis on functions rather than merely the position leads to greater employee loyalty and stronger relationships with your best customers.

Dierbergs Markets

Since Dierbergs, a 16-store chain in the St. Louis area, created a series of employee loyalty–based initiatives several years ago, annual turnover of the workforce has dropped from about 50 percent to a current 26 percent. Employing 4,000 unionized people, the company was faced with fewer than a dozen grievances in 1999. According to Fred Martels, senior human resources executive at Dierbergs, the vast majority of people leave, not because of pay or because they're not happy, but because of college or retirement.

To better understand the needs of their employees, extensive exit interviews were conducted with former employees. It was learned, for example, that people wanted to be in on things, not treated like a fifth wheel. Immediately, student and senior advisory councils were established to get input from employee groups. And although rules and regulations still have a part in the orientation process, a new emphasis is placed on fostering employee loyalty. New sign-ons now get a sizable diet of company traditions, including history and mission. They also learn of awards that have been bestowed on the company and see pictures of old stores and family members. A personalized packet of information goes to each employee with the person's name affixed.

When 55 percent of exit interviewees complained that employees had not learned enough about their jobs, the company taught workers about the products they sold and how customers should be served. This strategy stems in part from feelings of Generation X, whose members were born between 1965 and 1980 and need recognition, as they have an attitude about employment that they could be laid off tomorrow. To overcome this mentality, Dierbergs avoids assigning meaningless tasks, petty politics, and stereotyping while focusing on skill building. Like other leaders, Dierbergs is acutely aware that long-term customer satisfaction is intricately linked to building the right team.

EXCITE YOUR EMPLOYEES
FOR THE LONG TERM

Orientating, providing ongoing training, and offering upward mobility are the ways leading companies excite their employees. Smart firms focus on making employees comfortable with the functions of their employment during the orientation process. Leaders clearly identify the skills they want their employees to learn. Then they create a curriculum accompanied by a checklist to make sure the employees have attained the skill and knowledge required.

Following orientation, ongoing training is made a priority. Leaders keep their employees involved in a learning experience that gives them more skills and knowledge on a daily basis.

Land Rover North America

Land Rover's mission statement, "Our people are the band," reflects the company's belief that superior customer service gives Land Rover the edge it needs in the high-stakes game of high-adventure vehicles. Jim Newell, vice president of Land Rover University, says, "We want the customer to have a magical experience." To stimulate superior service, Land Rover implemented a program to train and retain employees for the long haul. The automaker created Land Rover University, where the classrooms are off-road training courses that give employees the chance to test out the vehicles. The idea was to instill loyalty in its staff, and year after year Land Rover receives an A with one of the best employee retention ratings in the automotive industry.

At Land Rover, the emphasis is on working together. Before opening a Land Rover Centre (exclusive retail outlets designed to look like hunting lodges), the entire sales team participates in a weeklong program. According to Newell, "The sales team includes absolutely everybody—down to the guy who washes the car." Land Rover's compensation structure also reflects its goal: It includes a base salary, a proportion of team sales, individual incentives, and customer service rewards.

"War stories," says Newell, "are the most valuable sales tools our employees possess. Imagine a sales rep discussing the features of a vehicle with a client, then pulling out a picture and saying, 'This is a photo of me when I did this.'" University events like Land Rover Trek, a multilevel competition between retailers, gives staffers stories to share. Trek emphasizes teamwork, pride in the product, and loyalty. For all this, Newell says, the cost of Trek is less than airing a TV commercial but just as valuable because "six months after it's over, the salespeople are still excited to sell."[1]

Upward mobility and incentives are the other tactics used by leaders to keep their employees excited.

Starbucks

An establishment such as Starbucks Corporation, a gourmet coffee purveyor, should weigh in with a 300 percent turnover—the figure for fast-food establishments, according to the National Restaurant Association. Starbucks core employees are predominantly under the age of 30—the age group with traditionally the least commitment to employers. But the company has a strikingly low 16 percent turnover of full-time employees and only a 60 percent turnover when part-timers are included.

"We've historically been in this range," says Jim Flanagan, Starbucks vice president of retail. "Our cafe atmosphere has a texture and a brand image that makes people comfortable working for us." Flanagan says his company sees no disadvantage in its youthful workers and believes it would be a mistake not to pursue them. Flanagan adds that when Starbucks started many of its benefits programs, the philosophy was that the frontline people were important and deserved these benefits. Besides the famous pound of coffee or tea a week, benefits offered to both full-time and part-time workers include a 30 percent employee discount, medical and dental coverage, a stock investment plan, and Bean Stock, the company's stock option plan. Still, even with all of these extra benefits, Flanagan believes that the company's culture is the underlying reason for its success. "It's tough out there with 4 percent unemployment and a shrinking workforce. Programs are critical, but we want to give people a 'different' place to work."[2]

Nordstrom

Nordstrom, the Seattle-based retailer, tries to attract people who want to earn substantial wages and creates an environment where they can. Joe Demarte, vice president of human resources, says that Nordstrom pays well and gives employees the opportunity to make even more money with its pay-for-performance commission system. "We have salespeople on the floor that made $100,000 last year," he notes.

Scheduling also rewards merit and ability; employees who rate high in sales and customer service get the busiest hours. These practices enable Nordstrom to build a staff that sticks around, even including part-timers; turnover is a very low 35 percent. Demarte adds, "We really believe that if we have salespeople who stay with us and build a relationship with customers, we'll also see a positive relationship to our sales and customer service."[3]

RECRUITMENT AS AN ONGOING PROCESS

Recruitment should be treated in the same way as marketing and sales are. Targeted campaigns need to be implemented to attract those people most likely to be interested in working with you. Maybe the best evidence is the fact that the vast majority of information technology (IT) jobs are found through the Internet, where IT people are most likely to spend a lot of their time. Microsoft and Intel receive thousands of hits a month on their Web sites as they actively seek to recruit new talent.

Leaders raise their visibility to these targeted groups. They do not hire people. Instead, they constantly look for key people to grow with their company. Recruiting must be focused on where you are going, not where you are.

Celestica

Within the high-tech community, one company that has effectively integrated a positive corporate culture into its daily operations is Fort Collins, Colorado–based Celestica Colorado, a subsidiary of Celestica, Inc., of Toronto. Operating under the assumption that happy employees are productive employees, which means satisfied customers, Celestica has placed a great deal of emphasis on creating a positive corporate culture. It specializes in electronic manufacturing and is one of the few firms where corporate culture is implemented, reworked, and exercised daily.

Mike Kelley, company communications manager who was with Hewlett-Packard before joining Celestica, is familiar with companies that aspire to corporate cultures that will attract and retain long-term employees. But he says that at Celestica, officials actually follow through with a stated commitment to teamwork, empowerment, technology, and process. "Our core value system forces us to stop and look at what we're supposed to be as a company," Kelley explains.

Celestica senior management, along with a group of employees, created the company's core values in 1996 at the headquarters office in Toronto. These values, which emphasize people, partnership, customer service, and quality, serve as a springboard for growth and highlight the importance of every employee and the value of quality work. Even though the values were created in 1996, they are described as a work in progress and continue to be managed and adjusted to meet the needs of employees.

In 1997 the company acquired the printed circuit board division of Hewlett-Packard in Fort Collins and has experienced exponential growth over the past three years. To date, Celestica has boosted production from 8 to 18 products, and the company is in the process of adding 9 manufacturing lines and nearly 1,000 jobs to raise the total number of full-time employees from 1,000 to 2,000. To ensure that the company's employees find deadlines fun and challenging, the company offers flexible work schedules and implements a recognition and rewards program for all departments. As a result, Celestica's attrition rates have been less than 1 percent for the last year. Says Kelley, "There's a lot of competition for talent, so we have to provide an environment that's enticing."[4]

Goelitz Candy

It may be a record, perhaps even a world record for the most jelly beans produced by any one company. The combined production of Jelly Belly jelly beans by Herman Goelitz Candy Company in Fairfield, California, and its affiliate Goelitz Confectionary Company in North Chicago, Illinois, is 100,000 pounds per day or 1,250,000 beans an hour. What is the most important influence behind Goelitz's record-setting production? Employee loyalty says Mike Bianco, vice president of plant operations. "We're very fortunate because we're well staffed with some great people who are very dedicated to the company. They like their jobs, and they work hard. The folks that have been with us for all these years and out on the line on a day-to-day basis give us a tremendous amount of input," Bianco says. Despite the stress of working months of overtime to fill orders that the North Chicago factory can't fill because of its sold-out status, employees in the California factory "want to see the next operation [the factory being built in Wisconsin] be the most technically advanced, the most efficient, and cleanest and neatest factory," says Bianco. However, even as automation constantly improves, Goelitz's employees, on whom the company relies for their expertise and loyalty, never have to fear that their jobs will be lost by the advancement of technologies. Says Bianco, "I can't remember a time when anyone lost their job because of automation. Anytime that we have automated, we have also expanded. Increased sales have allowed us to buy the equipment and keep all our people busy."[5]

SUMMARY

To develop effective, long-term relationships with their best and most profitable customers, leading companies viscerally realize they must also develop effective, long-term relationships with valuable employees who are able and willing to serve those customers.

Leading companies are the ones who have the right culture and procedures in place that enable them to identify, retain, and "grow" the right employees. Moreover, they are able to place their employees into the proper structure that allows the company to build the right team. Leaders build the right team by:

- Tailoring their people to the functions that support the execution of their system

- Exciting their employees about staying with them for the long term

- Recognizing that building a team is an ongoing process

CHAPTER 15

The Final Imperative

"What is the compelling reason your customers should do business with you?"

—Thom Winninger

The Shell representative looked out at his audience. It was made up of his company's top vendors, many of long standing and all of high repute. "I will take exactly three minutes of your time," he said, "because I have only three things to say.

"One, I want to congratulate all of you on your quality. Each of you should be proud of your products; we are. On a scale of 1 to 10, I would rank the quality of your products at or near a perfect 10.

"Two, I want to congratulate all of you on your service. Each of you should be proud of your service—we are. On the same scale of 1 to 10, I would rank each of you a 10 or close to it with regard to your service.

"Now, number three. In spite of the first two things I have said, we will probably not be doing business with 90 percent or more of you any longer. It is simply too expensive for us to send out dozens of requests for proposals, assess each one of them, negotiate them down cut by cut, and subsidize a large staff to spend its time on what has become essentially a repetitive operation. Even though all of you try hard to understand our business, none of you really knows it well enough—and it will get harder, not easier, as we grow here, downsize there, diversify into new businesses, and divest out of others—and we have no good way to teach it all to you, not the time, not the talent to devote to it, and not the inclination.

"As a result, we are going to choose one or two suppliers from each major category and make strategic alliances with them and take them deep into our business as our long-term partners. We will make our choices on the basis of which among you gives us the most compelling reason. Thank you."

"Wait!" everyone shouted at once. "What is the compelling reason?"

For the first time, the man from Shell smiled. "Now at last you're asking the right question."[1]

Like the suppliers at Shell, far too many companies in almost every industry imaginable have built their strategic planning around the idea that they can do it better than the competitors. Unfortunately, what too often happens is that well-intentioned companies and their leaders neglect their customers' real needs as well as the need to provide a truly customer-orientated service.

The airline industry is a perfect example of this failure of a process-oriented method of doing business. Once viewed as bold, romantic, and adventurous, like the Orient Express, air travel has become so dominated by process that it is no longer an experience. Today, airlines are ubiquitous and air travel is as commonplace as driving a car. Function and economics are what matter, not fulfilling customer expectations.

As a result, customers will probably choose a particular airline on the grounds of convenience and price rather than emotional responses to what the airline can offer them. For example, traveling business class versus economy class is normally a direct function of who is paying. Similarly, the choice of whether to fly one carrier over another is determined by the cost of the ticket and who arrives first. The end result is an entire industry in which most of the customers of almost every company in that industry view the product as mundane and ordinary at best.

With differences between airlines becoming almost nonexistent, it becomes difficult for customers to be discerning in their choices. Decisions, therefore, are based on the lowest common denominators—cost and convenience. Customer loyalty is something that seems unattainable. A distant dream.

But there is hope for the airlines and all other companies facing the same difficult and unpleasant situation. It is possible to set your products and services apart from the rest of the marketplace and successfully overcome the price wars that pervade most industries today. Many of the companies described in the previous pages here were able to stand out in crowded, seemingly homogeneous, industries by looking at themselves and, more important, their customers in completely new and revolutionary ways. They have realized that a strategic vision based on premium customer needs is the shortest and most effective path to building the lasting relationships all businesses are desperately seeking.

The way we live our lives is becoming the most important determinant to where, why, how, and when we buy things. Companies that will succeed in the future are those that understand lifestyle is becoming the key motivation behind purchasing decisions. Increasingly, customers are making their choices on the basis of how they perceive a product or service reflects their day-to-day life. Moreover, it is only when customers understand how a specific product or service fits within their lifestyle choices that is it possible to get full price. In today's world, the more a company is able to integrate itself with the real needs of its best customers, the easier it is to achieve full price for that company's products or services.

The imperatives discussed at length in the previous chapters are universal principles I observed while working with some of the finest companies across North America. They are intended to provide you with the tools your company will need as it builds those crucial relationships with your most profitable customers. Regardless of how the Internet changes the "stuff" of business, we will continue to buy products and services for the same reasons we did 20 years ago. Only those companies that view and use information technology as another tool, like each of the other imperatives described in this book, will be able to move toward the critical competitive advantage all of them are seeking.

Building your business around your best customers and their highest needs maximizes your value perception in the marketplace. Once your company is able to achieve Maximum Value Perception, then and only then will the notion of full price move from a mere fantasy to a certain reality.

ENDNOTES

Chapter 2: Leading the Field

1. Harvey Thompson, "What Do Your Customers Really Want?" *Journal of Business Strategy* (July/August 1998).
2. Ibid.
3. Henry Kim and David Mauborgne, "Getting It Done," *Brand Strategy* (October 1998).
4. Thompson.
5. Meryl Davids, "Not Exactly a Joyride at GM," *Journal of Business Strategy* (September/October 1998).
6. Kambiz Foroohar, "Rich Man, Poorer Man," *Forbes*, 24 March 1997.
7. Kim and Mauborgne.
8. Ibid.
9. "Retail Entrepreneurs of the Year," *Chain Store Age Executive* (December 1999).
10. Ibid.
11. Thompson.
12. Ibid.
13. Luisa Kroll, "Fear of Failing," *Forbes*, 24 March 1997.

Chapter 3: Selling the Program

1. Rick Mullin, "Taking Customer Relations to the Next Level," *Journal of Business Strategy* (January/February 1997).

2. James H. Gilmore and Joesph Pine III, "The Four Faces of Customization," *Harvard Business Review* (January/February 1997).

3. JoAnn Greco, "Retailing's Rule Breakers," *Journal of Business Strategy* (March/April 1997).

4. Gilmore and Pine.

5. Mullin.

6. Dwight Gertz, "Strategic Growth," *Journal of Business Strategy* (January/February 1996).

7. Ibid.

8. Ibid.

9. Stephen C. Miller, "Anybody in There? Sites Strain to Build In Customer Service," *New York Times,* 22 September 1999.

10. Ibid.

11. Ibid.

12. Peter Kolesar, Garrett van Rysin, and Wayne Cutler, "Creating Customer Value through Industrialized Intimacy," *Strategy & Business* (spring 1999).

13. Ibid.

14. Glenn Rifkin, "How Snap-On Tools Ratchets Its Brand," *Strategy & Business* (fall 1998).

15. Ibid.

Chapter 4: Vertical Integration

1. "Brink's Inc. Launches CompuSafe," *Convenience Store News,* 4 August 1997.

2. Donna Hood Crecca, "Beer and Pizza Promo 'In Store' for Chicago," *Supermarket News,* 10 March 1997.

3. "For Those Who Need to Brush," *Household & Personal Products Industry* (January 1999).

4. Al Heller, "Do-It-Yourself Health Care Boosts Sales in Home Diagnostics Category," *Drug Store News,* 6 October 1997.

5. Elizabeth Brent, "Drive-through Lumber Yards," *National Home Center News,* 24 November 1997.

6. Theresa Howard, "Gringo Honeymoon," *Brandweek,* 9 November 1998.

7. "Seven Seas Extra High Strength Pure Cod Liver Oil Liquid," *Brand Strategy* (January 1999).

Chapter 5: Segmenting Your Services to Targeted Customers

1. Scott Kirsner, "Dorothy Lane Loves Its Customers," *Chain Store News* (June 1999).
2. Becky Yerak, "Casino Companies Play Differently on the High-Roller Turf of Las Vegas," *Detroit News,* 9 March 1999.
3. "Grecian Sales Formula," *Golf Pro* 8 (June 1997).
4. "Fitness Craze of Aging Customers Fuels Sports Medicine," *Chain Drug Review,* 26 May 1997.
5. Jason Gonzalez, "Courting the Custom Builder," *National Home Center News,* 12 October 1998.
6. David Field, "Business Travelers Given Their Space: Leg Room Goes to Best United Fliers," *USA TODAY,* Money Section, 10 August 1999.
7. "Report Forecasts Hotel Room Boom," *Hotel & Management,* 14 December 1998.
8. M. A. Baumann, "Segmentation Creates More Niches," *Hotel and Motel Management,* 18 October 1999.
9. Ibid.
10. Ibid.
11. "Cheap Eats, Rich Flavors," *Restaurant Hospitality* (November 1999).

Chapter 6: Owning the Customer's Buying Cycle

1. Dick Silverman, "Consumers: Let Freedom Ring," *DNR,* 18 January 1999.
2. "Loyalty Promotion Boosts Top Tier Spending 20 Percent," *Customer Loyalty Today* (May 1999).
3. Ibid.
4. "Replay Program Arrives on Cue," *Customer Loyalty Today* (May 1999).
5. William J. McGee, "The Benefits of Membership," *Travel Agent,* 22 February 1999.
6. "Texas Chain Woos Sports Enthusiasts," *MMR,* 25 January 1999.
7. Richard Halverson, "Long-Life Products Multiply, May Endanger Repeat Sales," *Discount Store News,* 23 November 1998.

8. John Caulfield, "Lowe's Selling Strategies: Moving from Initiation to Motivation," *National Home Center News*, 14 December 1998.
9. "Loyal Family," *Incentive Today* (March 1999).

Chapter 7: Educating the Customer

1. Lillie Guyer and Laura Clark Geist, "Playing Piggyback," *Advertising Age*, 29 March 1999.
2. "Common Courtesy," *Footwear News*, 10 May 1999.
3. Kevin O'Rourke, "Targeting Consumer Education, Foot Care Tour Rolls Once More," *Drug Store News*, 7 June 1999.
4. Gordon Arnaut, "Internet Chat Rooms Becoming a Popular Forum for Business," *New York Times*, 26 January 1998.
5. Ibid.
6. "Online Shopping During Holiday Season Fuels Need for Consumer Education," *Business Wire*, 22 November 1999.
7. "PG&E Launches Summer Customer Energy Education Series," *Business Wire*, 25 June 1999.
8. Janet Moore, "A Giant Step for Red Wing Shoe," *Minneapolis Star Tribune*, 26 July 1999.

Chapter 8: Identifying Your Destination

1. "Bank One Sees International Product Gaps in Mid-Market," *International Banker*, 24 May 1999.
2. "Merck Comes Out on Top," *Med Ad News* (May 1999).
3. Michael Lafferty, "Inside American Express," *Bank Marketing International* (February 1999).
4. Sean Callahan, "Marketing Miracles," *Business Marketing*, 1 June 1999.
5. "Successful Introduction Leads Quikorder.com to Market Its Delivery Service Nationally," *PR Newswire*, 29 September 1999.
6. "SABRE Unveils Latest Offerings in Its Suite of Internet Solutions," *PR Newswire*, Fort Worth, Texas, 18 November 1999.
7. Laurence Zuckerman, "Corporations Betting That Computers Can Buy Productivity Gains," *New York Times*, 2 January 1997.

8. Edward Berryman, "Web Commerce: Be Prepared," *New York Times,* 12 October 1997.

9. Ibid.

10. Ibid.

11. "Toyota Motor Sales, USA to Grow Business-to-Business Sales with Entrance into E-Commerce," *Business Wire,* 30 September 1999.

12. "Online Mortgage Industry Poised for Explosive Growth," *PR Newswire,* 13 October 1999.

13. Ibid.

Chapter 9: Promoting Differences

1. Sonya Felix, "Got Any Loyalty?" *Canadian Business and Current Affairs* (August 1999).

2. Karen Klein, "Small Business: New Trends for Growing Companies," *Los Angeles Times,* 15 December 1999.

3. Tina Kyriakos, "Ritzman's Differentiation Comes Naturally," *Drug Store News,* 26 April 1999.

4. Susan Terry, "First Tennessee's FTB Online Plies the Internet," *Journal of Retail Banking Services,* 1 April 1999.

5. Melinda Fulmer, "Using Size to Their Advantage," *Los Angeles Times,* 10 November 1999.

6. "Farmer Jack Supermarkets' Accelerated Growth Strategy," *PR Newswire,* Detroit, Michigan, 3 December 1999.

7. John Case and Jerry Useem, "Coping with Change," *INC.* (March 1998).

Chapter 10: Substantiating Value, Not Price

1. Barry Sheehy, "Adding Value," *Executive Excellence* (July 1999).

2. Ibid.

3. Shari Cauldron, "Price War Draft Dodging," *Industry Week,* 5 January 1998.

4. Andrew E. Serwer, "How to Escape a Price War," *Fortune,* 13 June 1994.

5. Shari Caudron, "Ten Steps to Improve Customer Loyalty," *Industry Week: Growing Companies Edition* (October 1999).

6. "Mercedes-Benz USA and Its Retailers to Redefine Client Care," *PR Newswire*, Montvale, New Jersey, 14 September 1999.

Chapter 11: Living the Brand

1. Rochele Garner, "The Ties That Bind," *Sales and Marketing Management*, 1 October 1999.
2. Ibid.
3. Shelly Branch, "How Target Got Hot," *Fortune*, 24 May 1999.

Chapter 13: Forging the Indestructible System

1. Jeffrey Green, "Checkout Time for Cashiers," *Credit Card Management*, 1 November 1999.
2. Kimberly Lowe, "Combining Two Businesses and Two Systems," *National Petroleum News* (January 1997).
3. Don Peppers, "Don't Put Customer Relationships on Hold," *Sales and Marketing Management*, 1 September 1999.

Chapter 14: Building the Right Team

1. Brent Jordheim, "Success Secrets: Driving Home Training," *Sales and Marketing Management*, 1 September 1999.
2. Carla Johnson, "The Cost of Doing Business," *HR Magazine*, 1 December 1999.
3. Ibid.
4. Heather Grimshaw, "Celestica Nurtures Strong Corporate Culture Within," *Northern Colorado Business Report*, 16 July 1999.
5. "Goelitz's Fortunes Set by Employee Royalty," *Candy Industry*, 1 June 1998.

Chapter 15: The Final Imperative

1. Mack Hanan, "Tomorrow's Competition: The Next Generation of Growth Strategies," *AMACOM* (September 1993).

INDEX